*Consequential modifications of ss. 13 and 19 of
Children Act 1948*

Foster children

Inspection

PART III

MISCELLANEOUS AND GENERAL

Miscellaneous

Financial provisions

Supplemental

Children and Young Persons Act 1969

CHAPTER 54

ARRANGEMENT OF SECTIONS

A

Committal to care of local authorities

Transfer

*Consequential modifications of ss. 11 and 12 of
Children Act 1948.*

Detention

Legal aid

*Transitional modifications of Part I for persons of
specified ages*

Part II

Accommodation etc. for children in care, and foster children

Community homes

ELIZABETH II

1969 CHAPTER 54

An Act to amend the law relating to children and young
persons; and for purposes connected therewith.
[22nd October 1969]

B E IT ENACTED by the Queen's most Excellent Majesty, by
and with the advice and consent of the Lords Spiritual
and Temporal, and Commons, in this present Parliament
assembled, and by the authority of the same, as follows:—

PART I

CARE AND OTHER TREATMENT OF JUVENILES THROUGH COURT PROCEEDINGS

Care of children and young persons through juvenile courts

1.—(1) Any local authority, constable or authorised person
who reasonably believes that there are grounds for making an
order under this section in respect of a child or young person may,
subject to section 2(3) and (8) of this Act, bring him before a
juvenile court.

Care
proceedings
in juvenile
courts.

(2) If the court before which a child or young person is
brought under this section is of opinion that any of the following conditions is satisfied with respect to him, that is to say—

    (*a*) his proper development is being avoidably prevented or
neglected or his health is being avoidably impaired or
neglected or he is being ill-treated ; or

    (*b*) it is probable that the condition set out in the pre-
ceding paragraph will be satisfied in his case, having
regard to the fact that the court or another court has
found that that condition is or was satisfied in the case
of another child or young person who is or was a
member of the household to which he belongs ; or

    (*c*) he is exposed to moral danger ; or

A 3

(*d*) he is beyond the control of his parent or guardian ; or

(*e*) he is of compulsory school age within the meaning of the Education Act 1944 and is not receiving efficient full-time education suitable to his age, ability and aptitude ; or

(*f*) he is guilty of an offence, excluding homicide,

and also that he is in need of care or control which he is unlikely to receive unless the court makes an order under this section in respect of him, then, subject to the following provisions of this section and sections 2 and 3 of this Act, the court may if it thinks fit make such an order.

(3) The order which a court may make under this section in respect of a child or young person is—

(*a*) an order requiring his parent or guardian to enter into a recognisance to take proper care of him and exercise proper control over him ; or

(*b*) a supervision order ; or

(*c*) a care order (other than an interim order) ; or

(*d*) a hospital order within the meaning of Part V of the Mental Health Act 1959 ; or

(*e*) a guardianship order within the meaning of that Act.

(4) In any proceedings under this section the court may make orders in pursuance of paragraphs (*c*) and (*d*) of the preceding subsection but subject to that shall not make more than one of the orders mentioned in the preceding subsection, without prejudice to any power to make a further order in subsequent proceedings of any description ; and if in proceedings under this section the court makes one of those orders and an order so mentioned is already in force in respect of the child or young person in question, the court may discharge the earlier order unless it is a hospital or guardianship order.

(5) An order under this section shall not be made in respect of a child or young person—

(*a*) in pursuance of paragraph (*a*) of subsection (3) of this section unless the parent or guardian in question consents ;

(*b*) in pursuance of paragraph (*d*) or (*e*) of that subsection unless the conditions which, under section 60 of the said Act of 1959, are required to be satisfied for the making of a hospital or guardianship order in respect of a person convicted as mentioned in that section are satisfied in his case so far as they are applicable ;

(*c*) if he has attained the age of sixteen and is or has been married.

(6) In this section " authorised person " means a person authorised by order of the Secretary of State to bring proceedings in pursuance of this section and any officer of a society which is so authorised, and in sections 2 and 3 of this Act " care proceedings " means proceedings in pursuance of this section and " relevant infant " means the child or young person in respect of whom such proceedings are brought or proposed to be brought.

2.—(1) If a local authority receive information suggesting that there are grounds for bringing care proceedings in respect of a child or young person who resides or is found in their area, it shall be the duty of the authority to cause enquiries to be made into the case unless they are satisfied that such enquiries are unnecessary.

(2) If it appears to a local authority that there are grounds for bringing care proceedings in respect of a child or young person who resides or is found in their area, it shall be the duty of the authority to exercise their power under the preceding section to bring care proceedings in respect of him unless they are satisfied that it is neither in his interest nor the public interest to do so or that some other person is about to do so or to charge him with an offence.

(3) No care proceedings shall be begun by any person unless that person has given notice of the proceedings to the local authority for the area in which it appears to him that the relevant infant resides or, if it appears to him that the relevant infant does not reside in the area of a local authority, to the local authority for any area in which it appears to him that any circumstances giving rise to the proceedings arose ; but the preceding provisions of this subsection shall not apply where the person by whom the notice would fall to be given is the local authority in question.

(4) Without prejudice to any power to issue a summons or warrant apart from this subsection, a justice may issue a summons or warrant for the purpose of securing the attendance of the relevant infant before the court in which care proceedings are brought or proposed to be brought in respect of him ; but subsections (3) and (4) of section 47 of the Magistrates' Courts Act 1952 (which among other things restrict the circumstances in which a warrant may be issued) shall apply with the necessary modifications to a warrant under this subsection as they apply to a warrant under that section and as if in subsection (3) after the word " summons " there were inserted the words " cannot be served or ".

A 4

(5) Where the relevant infant is arrested in pursuance of a warrant issued by virtue of the preceding subsection and cannot be brought immediately before the court aforesaid, the person in whose custody he is—

    (a) may make arrangements for his detention in a place of safety for a period of not more than seventy-two hours from the time of the arrest (and it shall be lawful for him to be detained in pursuance of the arrangements) ; and

    (b) shall within that period, unless within it the relevant infant is brought before the court aforesaid, bring him before a justice ;

and the justice shall either make an interim order in respect of him or direct that he be released forthwith.

1952 c. 55.
(6) Section 77 of the Magistrates' Courts Act 1952 (under which a summons or warrant may be issued to secure the attendance of a witness) shall apply to care proceedings as it applies to the hearing of a complaint.

(7) In determining whether the condition set out in subsection (2)(b) of the preceding section is satisfied in respect of the relevant infant, it shall be assumed that no order under that section is to be made in respect of him.

(8) In relation to the condition set out in subsection (2)(e) of the preceding section the references to a local authority in that section and subsections (1), (2) and (11) (b) of this section shall be construed as references to a local education authority ; and in any care proceedings—

    (a) the court shall not entertain an allegation that that condition is satisfied unless the proceedings are brought by a local education authority ; and

    (b) the said condition shall be deemed to be satisfied if the relevant infant is of the age mentioned in that condition and it is proved that he—

        (i) is the subject of a school attendance order which is in force under section 37 of the Education Act 1944 and has not been complied with, or

1944 c. 31.

        (ii) is a registered pupil at a school which he is not attending regularly within the meaning of section 39 of that Act , or

        (iii) is a person whom another person habitually wandering from place to place takes with him,

    unless it is also proved that he is receiving the education mentioned in that condition ;

but nothing in paragraph (a) of this subsection shall prevent any evidence from being considered in care proceedings for any purpose other than that of determining whether that condition is satisfied in respect of the relevant infant.

(9) If on application under this subsection to the court in which it is proposed to bring care proceedings in respect of a relevant infant who is not present before the court it appears to the court that he is under the age of five and either—

(a) it is proved to the satisfaction of the court, on oath or in such other manner as may be prescribed by rules under section 15 of the Justices of the Peace Act 1949, 1949 c. 101. that notice of the proposal to bring the proceedings at the time and place at which the application is made was served on the parent or guardian of the relevant infant at what appears to the court to be a reasonable time before the making of the application ; or

(b) it appears to the court that his parent or guardian is present before the court

the court may if it thinks fit, after giving the parent or guardian if he is present an opportunity to be heard, give a direction under this subsection in respect of the relevant infant ; and a relevant infant in respect of whom such a direction is given by a court shall be deemed to have been brought before the court under section 1 of this Act at the time of the direction, and care proceedings in respect of him may be continued accordingly.

(10) If the court before which the relevant infant is brought in care proceedings is not in a position to decide what order, if any, ought to be made under the preceding section in respect of him, the court may make an interim order in respect of him.

(11) If it appears to the court before which the relevant infant is brought in care proceedings that he resides in a petty sessions area other than that for which the court acts, the court shall, unless it dismisses the case and subject to subsection (5) of the following section, direct that he be brought under the preceding section before a juvenile court acting for the petty sessions area in which he resides ; and where the court so directs—

(a) it may make an interim order in respect of him and, if it does so, shall cause the clerk of the court to which the direction relates to be informed of the case ;

(b) if the court does not make such an order it shall cause the local authority in whose area it appears to the court that the relevant infant resides to be informed of the case, and it shall be the duty of that authority to give effect to the direction within twenty-one days.

PART I

(12) The relevant infant may appeal to quarter sessions against any order made in respect of him under the preceding section except such an order as is mentioned in subsection (3)(*a*) of that section.

(13) Such an order as is mentioned in subsection (3)(*a*) of the preceding section shall not require the parent or guardian in question to enter into a recognisance for an amount exceeding fifty pounds or for a period exceeding three years or, where the relevant infant will attain the age of eighteen in a period shorter than three years, for a period exceeding that shorter period ; and section 96 of the Magistrates' Courts Act 1952 (which relates to the forfeiture of recognisances) shall apply to a recognisance entered into in pursuance of such an order as it applies to a recognisance to keep the peace.

1952 c. 55.

(14) For the purposes of this Act, care proceedings in respect of a relevant infant are begun when he is first brought before a juvenile court in pursuance of the preceding section in connection with the matter to which the proceedings relate.

Further supplementary provisions relating to s. 1(2)(*f*).

3.—(1) In any care proceedings, no account shall be taken for the purposes of the condition set out in paragraph (*f*) of subsection (2) of section 1 of this Act (hereafter in this section referred to as " the offence condition ") of an offence alleged to have been committed by the relevant infant if—

(*a*) in any previous care proceedings in respect of him it was alleged that the offence condition was satisfied in consequence of the offence ; or

(*b*) the offence is a summary offence within the meaning of the Magistrates' Courts Act 1952 and, disregarding section 4 of this Act, the period for beginning summary proceedings in respect of it expired before the care proceedings were begun ; or

(*c*) disregarding section 4 of this Act, he would if charged with the offence be entitled to be discharged under any rule of law relating to previous acquittal or conviction.

(2) In any care proceedings the court shall not entertain an allegation that the offence condition is satisfied in respect of the relevant infant unless the proceedings are brought by a local authority or a constable ; but nothing in this or the preceding subsection shall prevent any evidence from being considered in care proceedings for any purpose other than that of determining whether the offence condition is satisfied in respect of the relevant infant.

(3) If in any care proceedings the relevant infant is alleged to have committed an offence in consequence of which the offence

condition is satisfied with respect to him, the court shall not find the offence condition satisfied in consequence of the offence unless, disregarding section 4 of this Act, it would have found him guilty of the offence if the proceedings had been in pursuance of an information duly charging him with the offence and the court had had jurisdiction to try the information; and without prejudice to the preceding provisions of this subsection the same proof shall be required to substantiate or refute an allegation that the offence condition is satisfied in consequence of an offence as is required to warrant a finding of guilty, or as the case may be, of not guilty of the offence.

(4) A person shall not be charged with an offence if in care proceedings previously brought in respect of him it was alleged that the offence condition was satisfied in consequence of that offence.

(5) If in any care proceedings in which it is alleged that the offence condition is satisfied in respect of the relevant infant it appears to the court that the case falls to be remitted to another court in pursuance of subsection (11) of the preceding section but that it is appropriate to determine whether the condition is satisfied before remitting the case, the court may determine accordingly; and any determination under this subsection shall be binding on the court to which the case is remitted.

(6) Where in any care proceedings the court finds the offence condition satisfied with respect to the relevant infant in consequence of an indictable offence within the meaning of the Magistrates' Courts Act 1952 then, whether or not the court 1952 c. 55. makes an order under section 1 of this Act—

(a) section 34 of that Act (which relates to compensation for loss of property or damage to it) shall apply as if the finding were a finding of guilty of the offence and as if the maximum amount of an award under that section were one hundred pounds; and

(b) the court shall if the relevant infant is a child, and may if he is not, order any sum awarded by virtue of this subsection to be paid by his parent or guardian instead of by him unless it is satisfied that the parent or guardian cannot be found or has not conduced to the commission of the offence by neglecting to exercise due care or control of him, so however that an order shall not be made in pursuance of this paragraph unless the parent or guardian has been given an opportunity of being heard or has been required to attend the proceedings and failed to do so; and

     (c) any sum payable by a parent or guardian by virtue of the preceding paragraph may be recovered from him in like manner as if he had been convicted of the offence in question ;

but where the finding in question is made in pursuance of the preceding subsection, the powers conferred by this subsection shall be exercisable by the court to which the case is remitted instead of by the court which made the finding.

1914 c. 58.   For the purposes of this subsection an offence under section 14(1) of the Criminal Justice Administration Act 1914 (which provides for damage committed wilfully or maliciously to be punishable on summary conviction) shall be treated as an indictable offence within the meaning of the said Act of 1952.

(7) Where in any care proceedings the court finds the offence condition satisfied with respect to the relevant infant and he is a young person, the court may if it thinks fit and he consents, instead of making such an order as is mentioned in section 1(3) of this Act, order him to enter into a recognisance for an amount not exceeding twenty-five pounds and for a period not exceeding one year to keep the peace or to be of good behaviour ; and such an order shall be deemed to be an order under section 1 of this Act but no appeal to quarter sessions may be brought against an order under this subsection.

(8) Where in any care proceedings the court finds the offence condition satisfied with respect to the relevant infant in consequence of an offence which was not admitted by him before the court, then—

    (a) if the finding is made in pursuance of subsection (5) of this section and the court to which the case is remitted decides not to make any order under section 1 of this Act in respect of the relevant infant ; or

    (b) if the finding is not made in pursuance of that subsection and the court decides as aforesaid,

the relevant infant may appeal to quarter sessions against the finding, and in a case falling within paragraph (a) of this subsection any notice of appeal shall be given within fourteen days after the date of the decision mentioned in that paragraph ; and a person ordered to pay compensation by virtue of subsection (6) of this section may appeal to quarter sessions against the order.

(9) An appeal in pursuance of the preceding subsection or subsection (12) of the preceding section against an order made by a court in consequence of a finding made by another court by virtue of subsection (5) of this section shall lie to the same

quarter sessions as would have had jurisdiction to entertain
an appeal under subsection (8) of this section against the finding
if the court had decided not to make any order.

Consequential changes in criminal proceedings etc.

4. A person shall not be charged with an offence, except Prohibition of criminal proceedings for offences by children.
homicide, by reason of anything done or omitted while he was a
child.

5.—(1) A person other than a qualified informant shall not Restrictions on criminal proceedings for offences by young persons.
lay an information in respect of an offence if the alleged offender
is a young person.

(2) A qualified informant shall not lay an information in
respect of an offence if the alleged offender is a young person
unless the informant is of opinion that the case is of a description prescribed in pursuance of subsection (4) of this section
and that it would not be adequate for the case to be dealt with
by a parent, teacher or other person or by means of a caution
from a constable or through an exercise of the powers of a
local authority or other body not involving court proceedings
or by means of proceedings under section 1 of this Act.

(3) A qualified informant shall not come to a decision in
pursuance of the preceding subsection to lay an information
unless—

(a) he has told the appropriate local authority that the
laying of the information is being considered and has
asked for any observations which the authority may
wish to make on the case to the informant; and

(b) the authority either have notified the informant that they
do not wish to make such observations or have not
made any during the period or extended period indi-
cated by the informant as that which in the circumstances he considers reasonable for the purpose or the
informant has considered the observations made by the
authority during that period;

but the informant shall be entitled to disregard the foregoing
provisions of this subsection in any case in which it appears to
him that the requirements of the preceding subsection are satisfied and will continue to be satisfied notwithstanding any observations which might be made in pursuance of this subsection.

(4) The Secretary of State may make regulations specifying,
by reference to such considerations as he thinks fit, the descriptions of cases in which a qualified informant may lay an information in respect of an offence if the alleged offender is a young
person; but no regulations shall be made under this subsection
unless a draft of the regulations has been approved by a resolution of each House of Parliament.

(5) An information laid by a qualified informant in a case where the informant has reason to believe that the alleged offender is a young person shall be in writing and shall—

    (a) state the alleged offender's age to the best of the informant's knowledge ; and

    (b) contain a certificate signed by the informant stating that the requirements of subsections (2) and (3) of this section are satisfied with respect to the case or that the case is one in which the requirements of the said subsection (2) are satisfied and the informant is entitled to disregard the requirements of the said subsection (3).

(6) If at the time when justices begin to inquire into a case, either as examining justices or on the trial of an information, they have reason to believe that the alleged offender is a young person and either—

    (a) it appears to them that the person who laid the information in question was not a qualified informant when he laid it ; or

    (b) the information is not in writing or does not contain such a certificate as is mentioned in subsection (5)(b) of this section,

it shall be their duty to quash the information, without prejudice to the laying of a further information in respect of the matter in question ; but no proceedings shall be invalidated by reason of a contravention of any provision of this section and no action shall lie, by reason only of such a contravention, in respect of proceedings in respect of which such a contravention has occurred.

(7) Nothing in the preceding provisions of this section applies to an information laid with the consent of the Attorney General or laid by or on behalf or with the consent of the Director of Public Prosecutions.

(8) It shall be the duty of a person who decides to lay an information in respect of an offence in a case where he has reason to believe that the alleged offender is a young person to give notice of the decision to the appropriate local authority unless he is himself that authority.

(9) In this section—

    " the appropriate local authority ", in relation to a young person, means the local authority for the area in which it appears to the informant in question that the young person resides or, if the young person appears to the informant not to reside in the area of a local authority,

the local authority in whose area it is alleged that the
relevant offence or one of the relevant offences was
committed ; and

"qualified informant" means a servant of the Crown, a
police officer and a member of a designated police force
acting in his capacity as such a servant, officer or
member, a local authority, the Greater London Council,
the council of a county district and any body designated
as a public body for the purposes of this section ;

and in this subsection "designated" means designated by an
order made by the Secretary of State ; but nothing in this section
shall be construed as preventing any council or other body from
acting by an agent for the purposes of this section.

6.—(1) Where a person under the age of seventeen appears Summary
or is brought before a magistrates' court on an information trial of young
charging him with an offence, other than homicide, which is an persons.
indictable offence within the meaning of the Magistrates' Courts 1952 c. 55.
Act 1952, he shall be tried summarily unless—

    (a) he is a young person and the offence is such as is
mentioned in subsection (2) of section 53 of the Act of
1933 (under which young persons convicted on indictment of certain grave crimes may be sentenced to be
detained for long periods) and the court considers that
if he is found guilty of the offence it ought to be
possible to sentence him in pursuance of that subsection ; or

    (b) he is charged jointly with a person who has attained
the age of seventeen and the court considers it necessary
in the interests of justice to commit them both for
trial ;

and accordingly in a case falling within paragraph (a) or paragraph (b) of this subsection the court shall, if it is of opinion
that there is sufficient evidence to put the accused on trial,
commit him for trial.

(2) In sections 18(1) and 25(1) of the said Act of 1952 (which
provide for the trial on indictment of persons aged fourteen or
over who are charged with certain summary offences within
the meaning of that Act) for the word "fourteen" there shall
be substituted the word "seventeen".

(3) If on trying a person summarily in pursuance of subsection (1) of this section the court finds him guilty, it may
impose a fine of an amount not exceeding fifty pounds or may
exercise the same powers as it could have exercised if he
had been found guilty of an offence for which, but for section
107(2) of the said Act of 1952, it could have sentenced him to
imprisonment for a term not exceeding three months.

PART I
Alterations in
treatment
of young
offenders etc.
1948 c. 58.
1952 c. 55.

7.—(1) The minimum age at conviction which qualifies for a sentence of borstal training under section 20 of the Criminal Justice Act 1948 shall be seventeen instead of fifteen years ; and accordingly in subsection (1) of that section and section 28(1) of the Magistrates' Courts Act 1952 for the word "fifteen" there shall be substituted the word "seventeen".

(2) In section 3(1) of the said Act of 1948 (which authorises the court by or before which a person is convicted of an offence to make a probation order in respect of him) after the word "person" there shall be inserted the words "who has attained the age of seventeen".

1961 c. 39.

(3) If a court having power to order children or young persons of any class or description to be detained in a detention centre in pursuance of section 4 of the Criminal Justice Act 1961 or to attend at an attendance centre in pursuance of section 19 of the said Act of 1948 is notified in pursuance of this subsection by the Secretary of State that a detention centre or, as the case may be, an attendance centre will not be available for the reception from that court of children or young persons of that class or description after a date specified in the notification, the power in question shall not be exercisable by that court after that date ; and the Secretary of State shall cause a copy of any notification under this subsection to be published in the London Gazette before the date specified in the notification.

(4) Section 5 of the said Act of 1961 (which provides for detention for defaults) shall cease to apply to young persons.

(5) An order sending a person to an approved school shall not be made after such day as the Secretary of State may by order specify for the purposes of this subsection.

(6) Sections 54 and 57 of the Act of 1933 (which among other things enable a child or young person found guilty of an offence to be sent to a remand home or committed to the care of a fit person) shall cease to have effect.

(7) Subject to the enactments requiring cases to be remitted to juvenile courts and to section 53(1) of the Act of 1933 (which provides for detention for certain grave crimes), where a child is found guilty of homicide or a young person is found guilty of any offence by or before any court, that court or the court to which his case is remitted shall have power—

(a) if the offence is punishable in the case of an adult with imprisonment, to make a care order (other than an interim order) in respect of him ; or

(b) to make a supervision order in respect of him ; or

(c) with the consent of his parent or guardian, to order the parent or guardian to enter into a recognisance to take proper care of him and exercise proper control over him,

and, if it makes such an order as is mentioned in this subsection while another such order made by any court is in force in respect of the child or young person, shall also have power to discharge the earlier order ; and subsection (13) of section 2 of this Act shall apply to an order under paragraph (c) of this subsection as it applies to such an order as is mentioned in that subsection.

(8) Without prejudice to the power to remit any case to a juvenile court which is conferred on a magistrates' court other than a juvenile court by section 56(1) of the Act of 1933, in a case where such a magistrates' court finds a person guilty of an offence and either he is a young person or was a young person when the proceedings in question were begun it shall be the duty of the court to exercise that power unless the court decides to deal with the case by exercising a power to make one or more of the following orders, that is to say, an order discharging him absolutely or conditionally, an order for the payment of a fine, damages or costs, an order requiring his parent or guardian to enter into a recognisance to take proper care of him and exercise proper control over him or an order under section 5 or 7 of the Road Traffic Act 1962 (which relate respectively to the dis- 1962 c. 59. qualification of drivers and the endorsement of licences).

8.—(1) If a police officer not below the rank of inspector Finger-makes an application on oath to a justice stating— printing of

(a) that there is evidence sufficient to justify the laying of an suspected young information that a young person has or is suspected of persons. having committed an offence punishable with imprisonment in the case of an adult ; and

(b) that with a view to deciding, in accordance with section 5 of this Act, whether the information should be laid it is appropriate in the opinion of the officer for an order under subsection (2) of this section to be made in respect of the young person,

the justice may if he thinks fit issue a summons or warrant for the purpose of securing the attendance of the young person before a magistrates' court with a view to the making of such an order in respect of him.

(2) The court before which a young person appears in pursuance of a summons or warrant under the preceding subsection may if it thinks fit order his finger and palm prints to be taken by a constable.

PART I
1952 c. 55.

(3) Subsections (2) and (4) of section 40 of the Magistrates' Courts Act 1952 (which respectively relate to the taking and destruction of finger and palm prints) shall have effect as if references to an order under that section included references to an order under the preceding subsection and, in relation to an order under the preceding subsection, as if for the words from " remanded " to " committed " in subsection (2) there were substituted the words " lawfully detained at any place, at that place " and as if the reference to acquittal in subsection (4) included a reference to a finding of a court that the condition set out in section 1(2)(*f*) of this Act is not satisfied in consequence of the offence specified in the application mentioned in subsection (1) of this section.

Investigations
by local
authorities.

9.—(1) Where a local authority or a local education authority bring proceedings under section 1 of this Act or proceedings for an offence alleged to have been committed by a young person or are notified that any such proceedings are being brought, it shall be the duty of the authority, unless they are of opinion that it is unnecessary to do so, to make such investigations and provide the court before which the proceedings are heard with such information relating to the home surroundings, school record, health and character of the person in respect of whom the proceedings are brought as appear to the authority likely to assist the court.

(2) If the court mentioned in subsection (1) of this section requests the authority aforesaid to make investigations and provide information or to make further investigations and provide further information relating to the matters aforesaid, it shall be the duty of the authority to comply with the request.

Further
limitations on
publication of
particulars of
children and
young persons
etc.

10.—(1) In subsection (1) of section 49 of the Act of 1933 (which among other things imposes restrictions on reports of certain court proceedings concerning children or young persons but authorises the court or the Secretary of State, if satisfied that it is in the interests of justice to do so, to dispense with the requirements of that section)—

> (*a*) the references to a young person concerned in the proceedings as the person in respect of whom they are taken shall be construed as including references to any person who has attained the age of seventeen but not eighteen and against or in respect of whom the proceedings are taken and, in the case of proceedings under Part I of this Act, any other person in respect of whom those proceedings are taken ; and
>
> (*b*) the references to a juvenile court shall, in relation to proceedings in pursuance of the provisions of sections 15 and 16 of this Act or on appeal from such pro-

ceedings, be construed as including a reference to any
other magistrates' court or, as the case may be, the
court in which the appeal is brought ; and

(c) for the words " in the interests of justice so to do "
there shall be substituted the words " appropriate to
do so for the purpose of avoiding injustice to a child
or young person " and after the word " section " there
shall be inserted the words " in relation to him ".

(2) Where by virtue of paragraph (b) of the preceding
subsection the said section 49 applies to any proceedings, it
shall be the duty of the court in which the proceedings are taken
to announce in the course of the proceedings that that section
applies to them ; and if the court fails to do so that section shall
not apply to the proceedings in question.

(3) A notice displayed in pursuance of section 4 of the
Criminal Justice Act 1967 (which requires the publication of 1967 c. 80.
a notice stating the result of proceedings before examining
justices and containing particulars of the person to whom the
proceedings related) shall not contain the name or address of
any child or young person unless the justices in question have
stated that in their opinion he would be mentioned in the notice
apart from the foregoing provisions of this subsection and should
be mentioned in it for the purpose of avoiding injustice to him.

Supervision

11. Any provision of this Act authorising a court to make a Supervision
supervision order in respect of any person shall be construed as orders.
authorising the court to make an order placing him under the
supervision of a local authority designated by the order or of a
probation officer ; and in this Act " supervision order " shall be
construed accordingly and " supervised person " and " supervisor ", in relation to a supervision order, mean respectively the
person placed or to be placed under supervision by the order and
the person under whose supervision he is placed or to be placed
by the order.

12.—(1) A supervision order may require the supervised Power to
person to reside with an individual named in the order who include
agrees to the requirement, but a requirement imposed by a requirements in
supervision order in pursuance of this subsection shall be subject supervision
to any such requirement of the order as is authorised by the orders.
following provisions of this section.

(2) Subject to section 19(6) of this Act, a supervision order
may require the supervised person to comply with such directions
of the supervisor as are mentioned in paragraph (a) or (b) or
paragraphs (a) and (b) of this subsection, that is to say—

(a) directions requiring the supervised person to live for
a single period specified in the directions at a place
so specified ;

(b) directions given from time to time requiring him to do all or any of the following things—

(i) to live at a place or places specified in the directions for a period or periods so specified,

(ii) to present himself to a person or persons specified in the directions at a place or places and on a day or days so specified,

(iii) to participate in activities specified in the directions on a day or days so specified ;

but it shall be for the supervisor to decide whether and to what extent he exercises any power to give directions conferred on him by virtue of the preceding provisions of this subsection and to decide the form of any directions ; and a requirement imposed by a supervision order in pursuance of this subsection shall be subject to any such requirement of the order as is authorised by subsection (4) of this section.

(3) The periods specified in directions given by virtue of subsection (2) of this section in pursuance of a supervision order shall be in accordance with the following provisions, that is to say—

(a) the aggregate of the periods specified in directions given by virtue of paragraph (a) and paragraph (b) of that subsection shall not exceed ninety days ;

(b) the period specified in directions given by virtue of the said paragraph (a) shall not exceed ninety days and subject to paragraph (e) below shall not begin after the expiration of one year beginning with the date of the order or, if the directions are authorised solely by a variation of the order, with the date of the variation ;

(c) the aggregate of the periods specified in directions given by virtue of the said paragraph (b) shall not exceed thirty days in the year beginning with the date aforesaid and thirty days in any year beginning with an anniversary of that date ;

(d) if the order provides that any of the preceding paragraphs of this subsection is to have effect in relation to the order as if for a reference to ninety days or thirty days there were substituted a reference to a shorter period specified in the order, the paragraph in question shall have effect accordingly ;

(e) for the purpose of calculating the period or periods in respect of which directions may be given in pursuance of the order—

(i) the supervisor shall be entitled to disregard any day in respect of which directions were previously given in pursuance of the order and on which the directions were not complied with;

(ii) a direction given in respect of one or more parts of a day shall be treated as given in respect of the whole of the day,

and if during the year mentioned in paragraph (*b*) of this subsection the supervised person is given such directions as are there mentioned specifying a period beginning in that year but does not begin to comply with the directions during that year, the supervisor shall be entitled to disregard so much of that paragraph as prevents that period from beginning after the expiration of that year.

(4) Where a court which proposes to make a supervision order is satisfied, on the evidence of a medical practitioner approved for the purposes of section 28 of the Mental Health Act 1959, that the mental condition of a supervised person is such as requires and may be susceptible to treatment but is not such as to warrant his detention in pursuance of a hospital order under Part V of that Act, the court may include in the supervision order a requirement that the supervised person shall, for a period specified in the order, submit to treatment of one of the following descriptions so specified, that is to say— 1959 c. 72.

(*a*) treatment by or under the direction of a fully registered medical practitioner specified in the order;

(*b*) treatment as a non-resident patient at a place specified in the order; or

(*c*) treatment as a resident patient in a hospital or mental nursing home within the meaning of the said Act of 1959, but not a special hospital within the meaning of that Act.

(5) A requirement shall not be included in a supervision order in pursuance of the preceding subsection—

(*a*) in any case, unless the court is satisfied that arrangements have been or can be made for the treatment in question and, in the case of treatment as a resident patient, for the reception of the patient;

(*b*) in the case of an order made or to be made in respect of a person who has attained the age of fourteen, unless he consents to its inclusion;

and a requirement so included shall not in any case continue in force after the supervised person becomes eighteen.

13.—(1) A court shall not designate a local authority as the supervisor by a provision of a supervision order unless the authority agree or it appears to the court that the supervised person resides or will reside in the area of the authority.

Selection of supervisor.

PART I

(2) A court shall not insert in a supervision order a provision placing a child under the supervision of a probation officer unless the local authority of which the area is named or to be named in the order in pursuance of section 18(2)(*a*) of this Act so request and a probation officer is already exercising or has exercised, in relation to another member of the household to which the child belongs, duties imposed by paragraph 3(5) of Schedule 5 to the Criminal Justice Act 1948 or by rules under paragraph 6(*b*) of that Schedule.

1948 c. 58.

(3) Where a provision of a supervision order places a person under the supervision of a probation officer, the supervisor shall be a probation officer appointed for or assigned to the petty sessions area named in the order in pursuance of section 18(2)(*a*) of this Act and selected under arrangements made by the probation and after-care committee ; but if the probation officer selected as aforesaid dies or is unable to carry out his duties or if the case committee dealing with the case think it desirable that another officer should take his place, another probation officer shall be selected as aforesaid for the purposes of the order.

Duty of supervisor.

14. While a supervision order is in force it shall be the duty of the supervisor to advise, assist and befriend the supervised person.

Variation and discharge of supervision orders.

15.—(1) If while a supervision order is in force in respect of a supervised person who has not attained the age of eighteen it appears to a juvenile court, on the application of the supervisor or the supervised person, that it is appropriate to make an order under this subsection, the court may make an order discharging the supervision order or varying it by—

(*a*) cancelling any requirement included in it in pursuance of section 12 or section 18(2)(*b*) of this Act ; or

(*b*) inserting in it (either in addition to or in substitution for any of its provisions) any provision which could have been included in the order if the court had then had power to make it and were exercising the power,

and may on discharging the supervision order make a care order (other than an interim order) in respect of the supervised person ; but the powers of variation conferred by this subsection do not include power to insert in the supervision order, after the expiration of twelve months beginning with the date when the order was originally made, a requirement in pursuance of section 12(2)(*a*) of this Act or, after the expiration of three months beginning with that date, a requirement in pursuance of section 12(4) of this Act, unless in either case it is in substitution for such a requirement already included in the order.

(2) If on an application in pursuance of the preceding sub- PART I
section, in a case where the supervised person has attained the
age of seventeen and the supervision order was not made by
virtue of section 1 of this Act or on the occasion of the discharge
of a care order, it appears to the court appropriate to do so
it may proceed as if the application were in pursuance of subsection (3) or, if it is made by the supervisor, in pursuance of
subsections (3) and (4) of this section and as if in that subsection
or those subsections, as the case may be, the word " seventeen "
were substituted for the word " eighteen " and the words " a
magistrates' court other than " were omitted.

(3) If while a supervision order is in force in respect of a
supervised person who has attained the age of eighteen it appears
to a magistrates' court other than a juvenile court, on the application of the supervisor or the supervised person, that it is appropriate to make an order under this subsection, the court may
make an order discharging the supervision order or varying it
by—

  (*a*) inserting in it a provision specifying the duration of the
       order or altering or cancelling such a provision already
       included in it ; or

  (*b*) substituting for the provisions of the order by which
       the supervisor is designated or by virtue of which he is
       selected such other provisions in that behalf as could
       have been included in the order if the court had then
       had power to make it and were exercising the power ;
       or

  (*c*) substituting for the name of an area included in the
       order in pursuance of section 18(2)(*a*) of this Act the
       name of any other area of a local authority or petty
       sessions area, as the case may be, in which it appears
       to the court that the supervised person resides or will
       reside ; or

  (*d*) cancelling any provision included in the order by virtue
       of section 18(2)(*b*) of this Act or inserting in it any
       provision prescribed for the purposes of that paragraph ;
       or

  (*e*) cancelling any requirement included in the order in
       pursuance of section 12(1) or (2) of this Act.

(4) If while a supervision order is in force in respect of a
supervised person who has attained the age of eighteen it is
proved to the satisfaction of a magistrates' court other than a
juvenile court, on the application of the supervisor, that the
supervised person has failed to comply with any requirement

PART I included in the supervision órder in pursuance of section 12 or section 18(2)(*b*) of this Act, the court may—

> (*a*) whether or not it also makes an order under subsection (3) of this section, order him to pay a fine of an amount not exceeding twenty pounds or, subject to subsection (10) of the following section, make an attendance centre order in respect of him ;
>
> (*b*) if it also discharges the supervision order, make an order imposing on him any punishment which it could have imposed on him if it had then had power to try him for the offence in consequence of which the supervision order was made and had convicted him in the exercise of that power ;

and in a case where the offence in question is of a kind which the court has no power to try or has no power to try without appropriate consents, the punishment imposed by virtue of paragraph (*b*) of this subsection shall not exceed that which any court having power to try such an offence could have imposed in respect of it and shall not in any event exceed imprisonment for a term of six months and a fine of four hundred pounds.

(5) If a medical practitioner by whom or under whose direction a supervised person is being treated for his mental condition in pursuance of a requirement included in a supervision order by virtue of section 12(4) of this Act is unwilling to continue to treat or direct the treatment of the supervised person or is of opinion—

> (*a*) that the treatment should be continued beyond the period specified in that behalf in the order ; or
>
> (*b*) that the supervised person needs different treatment; or
>
> (*c*) that he is not susceptible to treatment ; or
>
> (*d*) that he does not require further treatment,

the practitioner shall make a report in writing to that effect to the supervisor ; and on receiving a report under this subsection the supervisor shall refer it to a juvenile court, and on such a reference the court may make an order cancelling or varying the requirement.

(6) The preceding provisions of this section shall have effect subject to the provisions of the following section.

Provisions supplementary to s. 15.   **16.**—(1) Where the supervisor makes an application or reference under the preceding section to a court he may bring the supervised person before the court, and subject to subsection (5) of this section a court shall not make an order under that section unless the supervised person is present before the court.

(2) Without prejudice to any power to issue a summons or warrant apart from this subsection, a justice may issue a summons or warrant for the purpose of securing the attendance of a supervised person before the court to which any application or reference in respect of him is made under the preceding section; but subsections (3) and (4) of section 47 of the Magistrates' Courts Act 1952 (which among other things restrict the circumstances in which a warrant may be issued) shall apply with the necessary modifications to a warrant under this subsection as they apply to a warrant under that section and as if in subsection (3) after the word " summons " there were inserted the words " cannot be served or ".

PART I

1952 c. 55.

(3) Where the supervised person is arrested in pursuance of a warrant issued by virtue of the preceding subsection and cannot be brought immediately before the court referred to in that subsection, the person in whose custody he is—

(*a*) may make arrangements for his detention in a place of safety for a period of not more than seventy-two hours from the time of the arrest (and it shall be lawful for him to be detained in pursuance of the arrangements); and

(*b*) shall within that period, unless within it the relevant infant is brought before the court aforesaid, bring him before a justice;

and the justice shall either direct that he be released forthwith or—

(i) if he has not attained the age of eighteen, make an interim order in respect of him;

(ii) if he has attained that age, remand him.

(4) If on an application to a court under subsection (1) of the preceding section—

(*a*) the supervised person is brought before the court under a warrant issued or an interim order made by virtue of the preceding provisions of this section; or

(*b*) the court considers that it is likely to exercise its powers under that subsection to make an order in respect of the supervised person but, before deciding whether to do so, seeks information with respect to him which it considers is unlikely to be obtained unless the court makes an interim order in respect of him,

the court may make an interim order in respect of the supervised person.

(5) A court may make an order under the preceding section in the absence of the supervised person if the effect of the order is confined to one or more of the following, that is to say—

(*a*) discharging the supervision order;

(b) cancelling a provision included in the supervision order in pursuance of section 12 or section 18(2)(b) of this Act;

(c) reducing the duration of the supervision order or any provision included in it in pursuance of the said section 12;

(d) altering in the supervision order the name of any area;

(e) changing the supervisor.

(6) A juvenile court shall not—

(a) exercise its powers under subsection (1) of the preceding section to make a care order or an order discharging a supervision order or inserting in it a requirement authorised by section 12 of this Act or varying or cancelling such a requirement except in a case where is unlikely to receive the care or control he needs the court is satisfied that the supervised person either unless the court makes the order or is likely to receive it notwithstanding the order;

(b) exercise its powers to make an order under subsection (5) of the preceding section except in such a case as is mentioned in paragraph (a) of this subsection;

(c) exercise its powers under the said subsection (1) to make an order inserting a requirement authorised by section 12(4) of this Act in a supervision order which does not already contain such a requirement unless the court is satisfied as mentioned in the said section 12(4) on such evidence as is there mentioned.

(7) Where the supervised person has attained the age of fourteen, then except with his consent a court shall not make an order under the preceding section containing provisions which insert in the supervision order a requirement authorised by section 12(4) of this Act or which alter such a requirement already included in the supervision order otherwise than by removing it or reducing its duration.

(8) The supervised person may appeal to quarter sessions against—

(a) any order made under the preceding section, except an order made or which could have been made in the absence of the supervised person and an order containing only provisions to which he consented in pursuance of the preceding subsection;

(b) the dismissal of an application under that section to discharge a supervision order.

(9) Where an application under the preceding section for the discharge of a supervision order is dismissed, no further application for its discharge shall be made under that section by any

person during the period of three months beginning with the
date of the dismissal except with the consent of a court having
jurisdiction to entertain such an application.

(10) In paragraph (*a*) of subsection (4) of the preceding section
" attendance centre order " means such an order to attend an
attendance centre as is mentioned in subsection (1) of section 19
of the Criminal Justice Act 1948 ; and the provisions of that
section shall accordingly apply for the purposes of that paragraph
as if for the words from " has power " to " probation order " in
subsection (1) there were substituted the words " considers it
appropriate to make an attendance centre order in respect of
any person in pursuance of section 15(4) of the Children and
Young Persons Act 1969 " and for references to an offender
there were substituted references to the supervised person and
as if subsection (5) were omitted.

(11) In this and the preceding section references to a juvenile
court or any other magistrates' court, in relation to a supervision
order, are references to such a court acting for the petty sessions
area for the time being named in the order in pursuance of
section 18(2)(*a*) of this Act; and if while an application to a
juvenile court in pursuance of the preceding section is pending
the supervised person to whom it relates attains the age of
seventeen or eighteen, the court shall deal with the application
as if he had not attained the age in question.

17. A supervision order shall, unless it has previously been
discharged, cease to have effect—

> (*a*) in any case, on the expiration of the period of three
> years, or such shorter period as may be specified in the
> order, beginning with the date on which the order was
> originally made ;
>
> (*b*) if the order was made by virtue of section 1 of this
> Act or on the occasion of the discharge of a care
> order and the supervised person attains the age of
> eighteen on a day earlier than that on which the
> order would expire under paragraph (*a*) above, on that
> earlier day.

18.—(1) A court shall not make a supervision order unless
it is satisfied that the supervised person resides or will reside
in the area of a local authority ; and a court shall be entitled
to be satisfied that the supervised person will so reside if he
is to be required so to reside by a provision to be included in
the order in pursuance of section 12(1) of this Act.

(2) A supervision order—

> (*a*) shall name the area of the local authority and the petty
> sessions area in which it appears to the court making

the order, or to the court varying any provision included in the order in pursuance of this paragraph, that the supervised person resides or will reside ; and

(b) may contain such prescribed provisions as the court aforesaid considers appropriate for facilitating the performance by the supervisor of his functions under section 14 of this Act, including any prescribed provisions for requiring visits to be made by the supervised person to the supervisor,

and in paragraph (b) of this subsection " prescribed " means prescribed by rules under section 15 of the Justices of the Peace Act 1949.

1949 c. 101.

(3) A court which makes a supervision order or an order varying or discharging a supervision order shall forthwith send a copy of its order—

(a) to the supervised person and, if the supervised person is a child, to his parent or guardian ; and

(b) to the supervisor and any person who has ceased to be the supervisor by virtue of the order ; and

(c) to any local authority who is not entitled by virtue of the preceding paragraph to such a copy and whose area is named in the supervision order in pursuance of the preceding subsection or has ceased to be so named by virtue of the court's order ; and

(d) where the supervised person is required by the order, or was required by the supervision order before it was varied or discharged, to reside with an individual or to undergo treatment by or under the direction of an individual or at any place, to the individual or the person in charge of that place ; and

(e) where a petty sessions area named in the order or discharged order in pursuance of subsection (2) of this section is not that for which the court acts, to the clerk to the justices for the petty sessions area so named ;

and, in a case falling within paragraph (e) of this subsection, shall also send to the clerk to the justices in question such documents and information relating to the case as the court considers likely to be of assistance to them.

(4) Where a supervision order requires compliance with such directions as are mentioned in section 12(2) of this Act, any expenditure incurred by the supervisor for the purposes of the directions shall be defrayed by the local authority of which the area is named in the order in pursuance of subsection (2) of this section.

19.—(1) It shall be the duty of the children's regional planning committee for each planning area (hereafter in this section referred to as " the committee ") to make arrangements, with such persons as the committee thinks fit, for the provision by those persons of facilities for enabling directions given by virtue of section 12(2) of this Act to persons resident in the area to be carried out effectively.

(2) The committee shall specify the arrangements made in pursuance of the preceding subsection in a scheme and shall submit the scheme to the Secretary of State for him to determine the date on which it is to come into force ; and the Secretary of State shall, after consultation with the committee and the relevant authorities, determine that date and notify his determination to the committee.

(3) On receiving a notification in pursuance of subsection (2) of this section in respect of a scheme, the committee shall send copies of the scheme and notification to each of the relevant authorities and to the clerk to the justices for each petty sessions area of which any part is included in the planning area in question ; and each of the relevant authorities shall, as soon as practicable after receiving those documents, keep a copy of them available at their principal offices for inspection by members of the public at all reasonable hours and on demand by any person furnish him with a copy of them free of charge.

(4) If, after the scheme prepared by the committee under this section has come into force, any arrangements specified in it are cancelled or the committee makes arrangements for the purposes of this section other than arrangements so specified, the committee shall send notice of the cancellations or other arrangements, stating the date on which they are to come into force and the alterations in the scheme which they entail, to the Secretary of State and the authorities and clerks mentioned in subsection (3) of this section ; and on and after that date the scheme shall have effect subject to those alterations and the relevant authorities shall have, in relation to the notice, the same duty as is imposed on them by that subsection in relation to the scheme.

(5) Arrangements in pursuance of this section shall not be made for any facilities unless the facilities are approved or are of a kind approved by the Secretary of State for the purposes of this section ; but where arrangements in pursuance of this section are made by the committee with any of the relevant authorities for the provision of facilities by the authority it shall be the duty of the authority to provide those facilities while the scheme is in force and those arrangements are specified in it.

(6) A court shall not include in a supervision order any such requirements as are mentioned in section 12(2) of this Act unless the court is satisfied that a scheme under this section is in force for the planning area in which the supervised person resides or will reside or that the date on which such a scheme is to come into force has been determined; and a supervisor authorised to give directions by virtue of any such requirements shall not, in pursuance of those requirements, give directions involving the use of facilities which are not for the time being specified in a scheme in force under this section for the planning area aforesaid.

Committal to care of local authorities

Orders for committal to care of local authorities.

20.—(1) Any provision of this Act authorising the making of a care order in respect of any person shall be construed as authorising the making of an order committing him to the care of a local authority; and in this Act " care order " shall be construed accordingly and " interim order " means a care order containing provision for the order to expire with the expiration of twenty-eight days, or of a shorter period specified in the order, beginning—

    (*a*) if the order is made by a court, with the date of the making of the order; and

    (*b*) if it is made by a justice, with the date when the person to whom it relates was first in legal custody in connection with the matter in consequence of which the order is made.

(2) The local authority to whose care a person is committed by a care order shall be—

    (*a*) except in the case of an interim order, the local authority in whose area it appears to the court making the order that that person resides or, if it does not appear to the court that he resides in the area of a local authority, any local authority in whose area it appears to the court that any offence was committed or any circumstances arose in consequence of which the order is made; and

    (*b*) in the case of an interim order, such one of the local authorities mentioned in paragraph (*a*) of this subsection as the court or justice making the order thinks fit (whether or not the person in question appears to reside in their area).

(3) Subject to the provisions of the following section, a care order other than an interim order shall cease to have effect—

    (*a*) if the person to whom it relates had attained the age of sixteen when the order was originally made, when he attains the age of nineteen; and (*b*) in any other case, when that person attains the age of eighteen.

(4) A care order shall be sufficient authority for the detention by any local authority or constable of the person to whom the order relates until he is received into the care of the authority to whose care he is committed by the order.

21.—(1) If it appears to a juvenile court, on the application of a local authority to whose care a person is committed by a care order which would cease to have effect by virtue of sub-section (3)(*b*) of the preceding section, that he is accommodated in a community home or a home provided by the Secretary of State and that by reason of his mental condition or behaviour it is in his interest or the public interest for him to continue to be so accommodated after he attains the age of eighteen, the court may order that the care order shall continue in force until he attains the age of nineteen ; but the court shall not make an order under this subsection unless the person in question is present before the court.

(2) If it appears to a juvenile court, on the application of a local authority to whose care a person is committed by a care order or on the application of that person, that it is appropriate to discharge the order, the court may discharge it and on discharging it may, unless it was an interim order and unless the person to whom the discharged order related has attained the age of eighteen, make a supervision order in respect of him.

(3) Where an application under the preceding subsection for the discharge of a care order is dismissed, then—

(*a*) in the case of an interim order, no further application for its discharge shall be made under that subsection except with the consent of a juvenile court (without prejudice to the power to make an application under subsection (4) of the following section) ; and

(*b*) in any other case, no further application for its discharge shall be made under this subsection by any person during the period of three months beginning with the date of the dismissal except with the consent of a juvenile court.

(4) The person to whom the relevant care order relates or related may appeal to quarter sessions against an order under subsection (1) of this section or a supervision order made in pursuance of subsection (2) of this section or the dismissal of an application under the said subsection (2) for the discharge of the care order.

(5) The local authority to whose care a person is committed by a care order (other than an interim order) may, within the period of three months beginning with the date of the order,

PART I appeal to quarter sessions against the provision of the order naming their area on the ground that at the time the order was made the person aforesaid resided in the area of another local authority named in the notice of appeal; but no appeal shall be brought by a local authority under this subsection unless they give notice in writing of the proposal to bring it to the other local authority in question before giving notice of appeal.

(6) References in this section to a juvenile court, in relation to a care order, are references to a juvenile court acting for any part of the area of the local authority to whose care a person is committed by the order or for the place where that person resides.

Special provisions relating to interim orders.

22.—(1) A juvenile court or a justice shall not make an interim order in respect of any person unless either—

(*a*) that person is present before the court or justice; or

(*b*) the court or justice is satisfied that he is under the age of five or cannot be present as aforesaid by reason of illness or accident.

(2) An interim order shall contain provision requiring the local authority to whose care a person is committed by the order to bring that person before a court specified in the order on the expiration of the order or at such earlier time as the specified court may require, so however that the said provision shall, if the court making the order considers it appropriate so to direct by reason of the fact that that person is under the age of five or by reason of illness or accident, require the local authority to bring him before the specified court on the expiration of the order only if the specified court so requires.

(3) A juvenile court acting for the same area as a juvenile court by which or a justice by whom an interim order has been made in respect of any person may, at any time before the expiration of the order, make a further interim order in respect of him; and the power to make an interim order conferred by this subsection is without prejudice to any other power to make such an order.

(4) The High Court may, on the application of a person to whom an interim order relates, discharge the order on such terms as the court thinks fit; but if on such an application the discharge of the order is refused, the local authority to whose care he is committed by the order shall not exercise in his case

1948 c. 43. their powers under section 13(2) of the Children Act 1948 (which enables them to allow a parent or other person to be in charge of him) except with the consent and in accordance with any directions of the High Court.

(5) If a court which has made or, apart from this subsection, would make an interim order in respect of a person who has attained the age of fourteen certifies that he is of so unruly a character that he cannot safely be committed to the care of a local authority and has been notified by the Secretary of State that a remand centre is available for the reception from the court of persons of his class or description, then, subject to the following provisions of this section, the court shall commit him to a remand centre for twenty-eight days or such shorter period as may be specified in the warrant; but in a case where an interim order is in force in respect of the person in question, a warrant under this subsection shall not be issued in respect of him except on the application of the local authority to whose care he is committed by the order and shall not be issued for a period extending beyond the date fixed for the expiration of the order, and on the issue of a warrant under this subsection in such a case the interim order shall cease to have effect.

In this subsection " court " includes a justice.

(6) Subsections (1), (3) and (4) of this section, so much of section 2(11)(*a*) as requires the clerk to be informed and section 21(2) to (4) of this Act shall apply to a warrant under subsection (5) of this section as they apply to an interim order but as if the words " is under the age of five or " in subsection (1) of this section were omitted.

23.—(1) Where a court—

Remand to care of local authorities etc.

   (*a*) remands or commits for trial a child charged with homicide or remands a child convicted of homicide ; or

   (*b*) remands a young person charged with or convicted of one or more offences or commits him for trial or sentence,

and he is not released on bail, then, subject to the following provisions of this section, the court shall commit him to the care of a local authority in whose area it appears to the court that he resides or that the offence or one of the offences was committed.

(2) If the court aforesaid certifies that a young person is of so unruly a character that he cannot safely be committed to the care of a local authority under the preceding subsection, then if the court has been notified by the Secretary of State that a remand centre is available for the reception from the court of persons of his class or description, it shall commit him to a remand centre and, if it has not been so notified, it shall commit him to a prison.

(3) If, on the application of the local authority to whose care a young person is committed by a warrant under subsection (1)

B

PART I

of this section, the court by which he was so committed or any magistrates' court having jurisdiction in the place where he is for the time being certifies as mentioned in subsection (2) of this section, the provisions of the said subsection (2) relating to committal shall apply in relation to him and he shall cease to be committed in pursuance of the said subsection (1).

1952 c. 55.

(4) The preceding provisions of this section shall have effect subject to the provisions of section 28 of the Magistrates' Courts Act 1952 (which relates to committal to quarter sessions with a view to a borstal sentence).

(5) In this section " court " and " magistrates' court " include a justice ; and notwithstanding anything in the preceding provisions of this section, section 105(5) of the said Act of 1952 (which provides for remands to the custody of a constable for periods not exceeding three clear days) shall have effect in relation to a child or young person as if for the reference to three clear days there were substituted a reference to twenty-four hours.

Powers and duties of local authorities etc. with respect to persons committed to their care.

24.—(1) It shall be the duty of a local authority to whose care a person is committed by a care order or by a warrant under subsection (1) of the preceding section to receive him into their care and, notwithstanding any claim by his parent or guardian, to keep him in their care while the order or warrant is in force.

(2) A local authority shall, subject to the following provisions of this section, have the same powers and duties with respect to a person in their care by virtue of a care order or such a warrant as his parent or guardian would have apart from the order or warrant and may (without prejudice to the preceding provisions of this subsection but subject to regulations made in pursuance of section 43 of this Act) restrict his liberty to such extent as the authority consider appropriate.

(3) A local authority shall not cause a person in their care by virtue of a care order to be brought up in any religious creed other than that in which he would have been brought up apart from the order.

(4) It shall be the duty of a local authority to comply with any provision included in an interim order in pursuance of section 22(2) of this Act and, in the case of a person in their care by virtue of the preceding section, to permit him to be removed from their care in due course of law.

(5) If a person who is subject to a care order and has attained the age of five is accommodated in a community home or other establishment which he has not been allowed to leave during the preceding three months for the purpose of ordinary

attendance at an educational institution or at work and it appears **PART I**
to the local authority to whose care he is committed by the
order that—

> (*a*) communication between him and his parent or guardian
> has been so infrequent that it is appropriate to appoint
> a visitor for him ; or
>
> (*b*) he has not lived with or visited or been visited by either
> of his parents or his guardian during the preceding
> twelve months,

it shall be the duty of the authority to appoint an independent
person to be his visitor for the purposes of this subsection ; and
a person so appointed shall—

> (i) have the duty of visiting, advising and befriending the
> person to whom the care order relates ; and
>
> (ii) be entitled to exercise on behalf of that person his powers
> under section 21(2) of this Act ; and
>
> (iii) be entitled to recover from the authority who appointed
> him any expenses reasonably incurred by him for the
> purposes of his functions under this subsection.

In this section " independent person " means a person satisfy-
ing such conditions as may be prescribed by regulations made by
the Secretary of State with a view to securing that he is independent of the local authority in question and unconnected with any
community home.

(6) A person's appointment as a visitor in pursuance of the
preceding subsection shall be determined if the care order in
question ceases to be in force or he gives notice in writing to the
authority who appointed him that he resigns the appointment or
the authority give him notice in writing that they terminate it ;
but the determination of such an appointment shall not prejudice
any duty under the preceding subsection to make a further
appointment.

(7) The functions conferred on a local authority by the preceding provisions of this section in respect of any person are in
addition to the functions which, by virtue of section 27 of this
Act, are conferred on the authority in respect of him by Part II
of the Children Act 1948.   1948 c. 43.

(8) While a care order other than an interim order is in
force in respect of a person who has not attained the age of
eighteen, it shall be the duty of his parent to keep the local
authority to whose care he is committed by the order informed
of the parent's address ; and if the parent knows of the order
and fails to perform his duty under this subsection, the parent
shall be liable on summary conviction to a fine not exceeding
ten pounds unless he shows that at the material time he was

residing at the address of the other parent and had reasonable cause to believe that the other parent had kept the authority informed of their address.

Transfer

Transfers
between
England or
Wales and
Northern
Ireland.

25.—(1) If it appears to the Secretary of State, on the application of the welfare authority or the managers of the training school to whose care a person is committed by a fit person order or by virtue of a training school order, that his parent or guardian resides or will reside in the area of a local authority in England or Wales, the Secretary of State may make an order committing him to the care of that local authority; and while an order under this subsection is in force it shall have effect as if it were a care order and as if sections 20(2) and (3) and 21(1) and (5) of this Act were omitted and in section 31(3)(*a*) of this Act for the reference to section 20(3) there were substituted a reference to subsection (3) of this section.

(2) If it appears to the Minister of Home Affairs for Northern Ireland, on the application of the local authority to whose care a person is committed by a care order other than an interim order, that his parent or guardian resides or will reside in Northern Ireland, the said Minister may make an order committing him to the care of the managers of a training school or to the care of the welfare authority in whose area his parent or guardian resides or will reside; and the provisions of the Children and Young Persons Act (Northern Ireland) 1968 (except sections 83(3)(*a*), 88(3), 90 and 91(3)) shall apply to an order under this subsection as if it were a training school order made on the date of the care order or, as the case may be, a fit person order.

1968 c. 34.
(N.I.).

If an order under this subsection commits a person to the care of the managers of a training school, the contributions to be made in respect of him under section 161 of the said Act of 1968 shall be made by such council as may be named in that order, being the council within whose district his parent proposes to reside or is residing at the time of the order.

(3) When a person is received into the care of a local authority or welfare authority or the managers of a training school in pursuance of an order under this section, the training school order, fit person order or care order in consequence of which the order under this section was made shall cease to have effect; and the order under this section shall, unless it is discharged earlier, cease to have effect—

(*a*) in the case of an order under subsection (1), on the earlier of the following dates, that is to say, the date when the person to whom the order relates attains the age of nineteen or the date when, by the effluxion of time, the

fit person order aforesaid would have ceased to have
effect or, as the case may be, the period of his detention
under the training school order aforesaid would have
expired;

(b) in the case of an order under subsection (2), on the date
when the care order aforesaid would have ceased to
have effect by the effluxion of time or—

(i) if the person to whom the order relates is
committed by it to the care of a welfare authority
and will attain the age of eighteen before that date,
when he attains that age;

(ii) if the order has effect by virtue of subsection (2)
as a training school order and the period of supervision following the detention of the person in
question in pursuance of the order expires before that
date, when that period expires.

(4) An order under this section shall be sufficient authority for
the detention in Northern Ireland, by any constable or by a
person duly authorised by a local authority or welfare authority
or the managers of a training school, of the person to whom the
order relates until he is received into the care of the authority or
managers to whose care he is committed by the order.

(5) In this section "training school", "training school
order" and "welfare authority" have the same meaning as in
the said Act of 1968, and "fit person order" means an order
under that Act committing a person to the care of a fit person.

26.—(1) The Secretary of State may by order designate for
the purposes of this section an order of any description which—

(a) a court in the Isle of Man or any of the Channel Islands
is authorised to make by the law for the time being in
force in that country; and

(b) provides for the committal to the care of a public
authority of a person who has not attained the age of
eighteen; and

(c) appears to the Secretary of State to be of the same nature
as a care order other than an interim order;

Transfers
between
England or
Wales and
the Channel
Islands or
Isle of Man.

and in this section "relevant order" means an order of a
description for the time being so designated and "the relevant
authority", in relation to a relevant order, means the authority
in the Isle of Man or any of the Channel Islands to whose care
the person to whom the order relates is, under the law of that
country, committed by the order.

(2) The Secretary of State may authorise a local authority to
receive into their care any person named in the authorisation who
is the subject of a relevant order; and while such an authorisa-

PART I

tion is in force in respect of any person he shall, subject to the following subsection, be deemed to be the subject of a care order committing him to the care of the local authority.

(3) This Act shall have effect, in relation to a person in respect of whom an authorisation under this section is in force, as if sections 20(2) and (3), 21 and 31 and in section 27(4) the words from " and if " onwards were omitted ; and it shall be the duty of a local authority who propose, in exercise of their powers under section 13(2) of the Children Act 1948, to allow such a person to be under the charge and control of a person residing outside England and Wales to consult the relevant authority before exercising those powers.

1948 c. 43.

(4) An authorisation given to a local authority under this section shall cease to have effect when—

(a) the local authority is informed by the Secretary of State that he has revoked it ; or

(b) the relevant order to which the authorisation relates ceases to have effect by the effluxion of time under the law of the place where the order was made or the local authority is informed by the relevant authority that the order has been discharged under that law ; or

(c) the person to whom the relevant order relates is again received into the care of the relevant authority ;

and if a local authority having by virtue of this section the care of a person to whom a relevant order relates is requested by the relevant authority to make arrangements for him to be received again into the care of the relevant authority, it shall be the duty of the local authority to comply with the request.

Consequential modifications of ss. 11 *and* 12 *of*
Children Act 1948

Consequential modifications of 1948 c. 43 s.s. 11 and 12.

27.—(1) For section 11 of the Children Act 1948 (which specifies the children in respect of whom functions are conferred on local authorities by Part II of that Act) there shall be substituted the following section : —

Children to whom Part II applies.

11. Except where the contrary intention appears, any reference in this Part of this Act to a child who is or was in the care of a local authority is a reference to a child who is or was in the care of the authority under section 1 of this Act or by virtue of a care order within the meaning of the Children and Young Persons Act 1969 or a warrant under section 23(1) of that Act (which relates to remands in the care of local authorities). ;

but nothing in the said section 11 as replaced by this subsection prejudices the application of any provision of the said **Part II** to any person by virtue of an enactment passed after that Act and before this Act.

(2) If it appears to a local authority that it is necessary, for the purpose of protecting members of the public, to exercise their powers in relation to a particular child in their care in a manner which may not be consistent with their general duty under section 12(1) of the said Act of 1948 to further his best interests and afford him opportunity for proper development, the authority may, notwithstanding that duty, act in that manner.

(3) If the Secretary of State considers it necessary, for the purpose of protecting members of the public, to give directions to a local authority with respect to the exercise of their powers in relation to a particular child in their care, he may give such directions to the authority ; and it shall be the duty of the authority, notwithstanding their general duty aforesaid, to comply with any such directions.

(4) Without prejudice to their general duty aforesaid, it shall be the duty of a local authority who have at any time had a child in their care throughout the preceding six months and have not during that period held a review of his case in pursuance of this subsection to review his case as soon as is practicable after the expiration of that period and, if a care order is in force with respect to him, to consider in the course of the review whether to make an application for the discharge of the order.

Detention

28.—(1) If, upon an application to a justice by any person for authority to detain a child or young person and take him to a place of safety, the justice is satisfied that the applicant has reasonable cause to believe that—

Detention of child or young person in place of safety.

 (*a*) any of the conditions set out in section 1(2)(*a*) to (*e*) of this Act is satisfied in respect of the child or young person ; or

 (*b*) an appropriate court would find the condition set out in section 1(2)(*b*) of this Act satisfied in respect of him ; or

 (*c*) the child or young person is about to leave the United Kingdom in contravention of section 25 of the Act of 1933 (which regulates the sending abroad of juvenile entertainers),

the justice may grant the application ; and the child or young person in respect of whom an authorisation is issued under this subsection may be detained in a place of safety by virtue of the

PART I authorisation for twenty-eight days beginning with the date of authorisation, or for such shorter period beginning with that date as may be specified in the authorisation.

(2) Any constable may detain a child or young person as respects whom the constable has reasonable cause to believe that any of the conditions set out in section 1(2)(a) to (d) of this Act is satisfied or that an appropriate court would find the condition set out in section 1(2)(b) of this Act satisfied or that an offence is being committed under section 10(1) of the Act of 1933 (which penalises a vagrant who takes a juvenile from place to place).

(3) A person who detains any person in pursuance of the preceding provisions of this section shall, as soon as practicable after doing so, inform him of the reason for his detention and take such steps as are practicable for informing his parent or guardian of his detention and of the reason for it.

(4) A constable who detains any person in pursuance of subsection (2) of this section or who arrests a child without a warrant otherwise than for homicide shall as soon as practicable after doing so secure that the case is enquired into by a police officer not below the rank of inspector or by the police officer in charge of a police station, and that officer shall on completing the enquiry either—

    (a) release the person in question ; or

    (b) if the officer considers that he ought to be further detained in his own interests or, in the case of an arrested child, because of the nature of the alleged offence, make arrangements for his detention in a place of safety and inform him, and take such steps as are practicable for informing his parent or guardian, of his right to apply to a justice under subsection (5) of this section for his release ;

and subject to the said subsection (5) it shall be lawful to detain the person in question in accordance with any such arrangements.

(5) It shall not be lawful for a child arrested without a warrant otherwise than for homicide to be detained in consequence of the arrest or such arrangements as aforesaid, or for any person to be detained by virtue of subsection (2) of this section or any such arrangements, after the expiration of the period of eight days beginning with the day on which he was arrested or, as the case may be, on which his detention in pursuance of the said subsection (2) began ; and if during that period the person in question applies to a justice for his release, the justice shall direct that he be released forthwith unless the justice considers

that he ought to be further detained in his own interests or, in the case of an arrested child, because of the nature of the alleged offence.

(6) If while a person is detained in pursuance of this section an application for an interim order in respect of him is made to a magistrates' court or a justice, the court or justice shall either make or refuse to make the order and, in the case of a refusal, may direct that he be released forthwith.

29.—(1) Where a person is arrested with or without a warrant and cannot be brought immediately before a magistrates' court, then if either—

    (*a*) he appears to be a child and his arrest is for homicide ; or

    (*b*) he appears to be a young person and his arrest is for any offence,

the police officer in charge of the police station to which he is brought or another police officer not below the rank of inspector shall forthwith enquire into the case and, subject to subsection (2) of this section, shall release him unless—

    (i) the officer considers that he ought in his own interests to be further detained ; or

    (ii) the officer has reason to believe that he has committed homicide or another grave crime or that his release would defeat the ends of justice or that if he were released (in a case where he was arrested without a warrant) he would fail to appear to answer to any charge which might be made.

(2) A person arrested in pursuance of a warrant shall not be released in pursuance of subsection (1) of this section unless he or his parent or guardian (with or without sureties) enters into a recognisance for such amount as the officer aforesaid considers will secure his attendance at the hearing of the charge ; and a recognisance entered into in pursuance of this subsection may, if the said officer thinks fit, be conditioned for the attendance of the parent or guardian at the hearing in addition to the person arrested.

(3) An officer who enquires into a case in pursuance of subsection (1) of this section and does not release the person to whom the enquiry relates shall, unless the officer certifies that it is impracticable to do so or that he is of so unruly a character as to make it inappropriate to do so, make arrangements for him to be taken into the care of a local authority and detained by the authority, and it shall be lawful to detain him in pursuance of the arrangements ; and a certificate made under this subsection in respect of any person shall be produced to the court before which that person is first brought thereafter

(4) Where an officer decides in pursuance of subsection (1) of this section not to release a person arrested without a warrant and it appears to the officer that a decision falls to be taken in pursuance of section 5 of this Act whether to lay an information in respect of an offence alleged to have been committed by that person, it shall be the duty of the officer to inform him that such a decision falls to be taken and to specify the offence.

(5) A person detained by virtue of subsection (3) of this section shall be brought before a magistrates' court within seventy-two hours from the time of his arrest unless within that period a police officer not below the rank of inspector certifies to a magistrates' court that by reason of illness or accident he cannot be brought before a magistrates' court within that period.

(6) Where in pursuance of the preceding subsection a person is brought before a court or a certificate in respect of any person is produced to a court and the court does not proceed forthwith to inquire into the case, then—

(a) except in a case falling within paragraph (b) of this subsection, the court shall order his release; and

(b) in a case where he was arrested in pursuance of a warrant or the court considers that he ought in his own interests to be further detained or the court has reason to believe as mentioned in subsection (1)(ii) of this section, the court shall remand him;

and where a court remands a person in pursuance of this subsection otherwise than on bail it shall, if he is not represented by counsel or a solicitor, inform him that he may apply to a judge of the High Court to be admitted to bail and shall, if he is not so represented or his counsel or solicitor so requests, give him a written notice stating the reason for so remanding him.

Detention of young offenders in community homes.

30.—(1) The power to give directions under section 53 of the Act of 1933 (under which young offenders convicted on indictment of certain grave crimes may be detained in accordance with directions given by the Secretary of State) shall include power to direct detention by a local authority specified in the directions in a home so specified which is a community home provided by the authority or a controlled community home for the management, equipment and maintenance of which the authority are responsible; but a person shall not be liable to be detained in the manner provided by this section after he attains the age of nineteen.

(2) It shall be the duty of a local authority specified in directions given in pursuance of this section to detain the person to whom the directions relate in the home specified in the

directions subject to and in accordance with such instructions
relating to him as the Secretary of State may give to the
authority from time to time ; and the authority shall be entitled
to recover from the Secretary of State any expenses reasonably
incurred by them in discharging that duty.

PART I

31.—(1) Where a person who has attained the age of fifteen
is for the time being committed to the care of a local authority
by a care order (other than an interim order) and accommodated
in a community home and the authority consider that he ought
to be removed to a borstal institution under this section, they
may with the consent of the Secretary of State bring him before
a juvenile court.

Removal to
borstal
institutions of
persons
committed to
care of local
authorities.

(2) If the court before which a person is brought in pursuance
of this section is satisfied that his behaviour is such that it will
be detrimental to the persons accommodated in any community
home for him to be accommodated there, the court may order
him to be removed to a borstal institution.

(3) Where an order is made under subsection (2) of this
section with respect to any person, the care order aforesaid
shall cease to have effect and he shall be treated as if he had
been sentenced to borstal training on the date of the other
order, except that—

> (a) where the day on which the care order would have
> ceased to have effect by virtue of section 20(3) of
> this Act (disregarding section 21(1)) is earlier than the
> end of the period of two years beginning with the date
> aforesaid he shall, subject to paragraph (b) of this
> subsection, not be liable to be detained by virtue of this
> subsection after that day ; and

> (b) section 45(4) of the Prison Act 1952 shall apply to him
> as if for the reference to two years from the date of his
> sentence there were substituted a reference to that
> day.

1952 c. 52

(4) If the court before which a person is brought in pursuance
of this section is not in a position to decide whether to make
an order under subsection (2) of this section in respect of him,
it may make an order for his detention in a remand centre for a
period not exceeding twenty-one days.

(5) An order under the preceding subsection may from time
to time be varied or extended by the court which made the order
or by any other magistrates' court acting for the same area as
that court, but a court shall not exercise its powers under this
subsection—

> (a) if the person to whom the order relates is not before
> the court, unless the court is satisfied that by reason
> of illness or accident he cannot be present ;

PART I

1952 c. 55.

    (*b*) so as to authorise the detention of that person after the expiration of the period of eight weeks beginning with the date when the order was originally made.

    (6) The provisions of the Magistrates' Courts Act 1952 and of any other enactment relating to summary proceedings (other than provisions relating to remand or legal aid) shall apply to proceedings for the removal of a person under this section as they apply to proceedings against a person charged with a summary offence.

    (7) Where immediately before an order under paragraph (*f*) of section 34(1) of this Act comes into force an order under this section is in force with respect to any person, the order under that paragraph shall not affect the other order or the application of this section to that person while the other order remains in force.

Detention of absentees.

1968 c. 34. (N.I.).

    32.—(1) If any of the following persons, that is to say—

    (*a*) a person committed to the care of a local authority by a care order or by a warrant under section 23 of this Act ; or

    (*b*) a person who, in pursuance of section 2(5), 16(3) or 28 of this Act, has been taken to a place of safety which is a community home provided by a local authority or a controlled community home ; or

    (*c*) a person in the care of a local authority in pursuance of arrangements under section 29(3) of this Act ; or

    (*d*) a person sent to a remand home, special reception centre or training school or committed to the care of a fit person under the Children and Young Persons Act (Northern Ireland) 1968,

is absent from premises at which he is required by the local authority or the relevant Northern Ireland authority to live, or as the case may be is absent from the home, remand home, special reception centre or training school, at a time when he is not permitted by the local authority or the managers of the home or the relevant Northern Ireland authority to be absent from it, he may be arrested by a constable anywhere in the United Kingdom or the Channel Islands without a warrant and shall if so arrested be conducted, at the expense of the authority or managers, to the premises or other place aforesaid or such other premises as the authority or managers may direct.

    (2) If a magistrates' court is satisfied by information on oath that there are reasonable grounds for believing that a person specified in the information can produce a person who is absent as mentioned in subsection (1) of this section, the court may issue a summons directed to the person so specified and requiring him to attend and produce the absent person before the court ; and a person who without reasonable excuse fails

to comply with any such requirement shall, without prejudice to PART I
any liability apart from this subsection, be guilty of an offence
and liable on summary conviction to a fine of an amount not
exceeding twenty pounds.

In the application of this subsection to Northern Ireland,
" magistrates' court " means a magistrates' court within the 1964 c. 21
meaning of the Magistrates' Courts Act (Northern Ireland) 1964. (N.I.).

(3) A person who knowingly compels, persuades, incites or
assists another person to become or continue to be absent as
mentioned in subsection (1) of this section shall be guilty of an
offence and liable on summary conviction to imprisonment for
a term not exceeding six months or a fine of an amount not
exceeding one hundred pounds or both.

(4) The reference to a constable in subsection (1) of this
section includes a reference to a person who is a constable
under the law of any part of the United Kingdom, to a member
of the police in Jersey and to an officer of police within the
meaning of section 43 of the Larceny (Guernsey) Law 1958 or
any corresponding law for the time being in force, and in that
subsection " the relevant Northern Ireland authority " means
in the case of a person committed to the care of a fit person, the
fit person, and in the case of a person sent to a remand home,
special reception centre or training school, the person in charge
of that home or centre or the managers of that school.

(5) Nothing in this section authorises the arrest in Northern
Ireland of, or the taking there of any proceedings in respect of,
such a person as is mentioned in paragraph (d) of subsection (1)
of this section.

Legal aid

33.—(1) Part IV of the Criminal Justice Act 1967 (which Legal aid.
relates to legal aid in criminal proceedings) shall have effect 1967 c. 80.
subject to the provisions of Schedule 1 to this Act (being provisions for applying the said Part IV to certain proceedings
under this Part of this Act and for modifying the said Part IV
in certain minor respects in relation to juveniles).

(2) Legal aid in pursuance of the Legal Aid and Advice 1949 c. 51.
Act 1949 shall not be given in respect of any proceedings in
respect of which legal aid may be given by virtue of the preceding subsection.

*Transitional modifications of Part 1 for
persons of specified ages*

Transitional
modifications
of Part I for
persons of
specified ages.

34.—(1) The Secretary of State may by order provide—

(a) that any reference to a child in section 4, 13(2) or 28(4)
or (5) of this Act shall be construed as excluding a
child who has attained such age as may be specified in
the order ;

(b) that any reference to a young person in section 5 of
this Act (except subsection (8)) shall be construed
as including a child, or excluding a young person,
who has attained such age as may be so specified ;

(c) that any reference to a young person in section 5(8),
7(7), 7(8), 9(1), 23(1) or 29(1) of this Act shall be
construed as including a child who has attained such
age as may be so specified ;

(d) that section 7(1) of this Act shall have effect as if for
references to seventeen years there were substituted
references to sixteen years ;

(e) that section 23(2) or (3) of this Act shall have effect
as if the references to a young person excluded a
young person who has not attained such age as may be
so specified ;

(f) that section 22(5) of this Act shall have effect as if for
the reference to the age of fourteen, or section 31(1)
of this Act shall have effect as if for the reference to
the age of fifteen, there were substituted a reference
to such greater age as may be so specified.

(2) In the case of a person who has not attained the age of
seventeen but has attained such lower age as the Secretary of
State may by order specify, no proceedings under section 1 of
this Act or for an offence shall be begun in any court unless
the person proposing to begin the proceedings has, in addition
to any notice falling to be given by him to a local authority
in pursuance of section 2(3) or 5(8) of this Act, given notice
of the proceedings to a probation officer for the area for
which the court acts ; and accordingly in the case of such a
person the reference in section 1(1) of this Act to the said section
2(3) shall be construed as including a reference to this subsection.

(3) In the case of a person who has attained such age as the
Secretary of State may by order specify, an authority shall,
without prejudice to subsection (2) of section 9 of this Act,
not be required by virtue of subsection (1) of that section to
make investigations or provide information which it does not
already possess with respect to his home surroundings if, by
direction of the justices or probation and after-care committee

acting for any relevant area, arrangements are in force for information with respect to his home surroundings to be furnished to the court in question by a probation officer.

(4) Except in relation to section 13(2) of this Act, references to a child in subsection (1) of this section do not include references to a person under the age of ten.

(5) In relation to a child tried summarily in pursuance of section 6 of this Act, for the words " fifty pounds " in subsection (3) of that section there shall be substituted the words " ten pounds ".

(6) Without prejudice to the generality of section 69(4) of this Act, an order under this section may specify different ages for the purposes of different provisions of this Act specified in the order.

(7) A draft of any order proposed to be made under this section shall be laid before Parliament and, in the case of an order of which the effect is that the reference to a child in section 4 of this Act includes a child who has attained an age of more than twelve, shall not be made unless the draft has been approved by a resolution of each House of Parliament.

PART II

ACCOMMODATION ETC. FOR CHILDREN IN CARE, AND FOSTER CHILDREN

Community homes

35.—(1) With a view to the preparation, in pursuance of the provisions of this Part of this Act, of regional plans for the provision of accommodation for children in the care of local authorities and for the equipment and maintenance of the accommodation, the Secretary of State may by order provide that any area specified in the order shall be a separate area (in this Act referred to as a " planning area ") for the purposes of those provisions.

Regional planning of accommodation for children in care.

(2) Before making an order under subsection (1) of this section, the Secretary of State shall consult each local authority whose area or any part of whose area is included in the planning area which he proposes should be specified in the order and such other local authorities, if any, as he thinks fit.

(3) It shall be the duty of the local authorities whose areas are wholly or partly included in a planning area (in this Act referred to, in relation to such an area, as " the relevant authorities ") to establish for the area, within such period as may be provided by the order specifying the planning area or such longer period as the Secretary of State may allow, a body to be called the children's regional planning committee.

PART II   (4) The provisions of Schedule 2 to this Act shall have effect in relation to children's regional planning committees.

(5) In the case of an order under subsection (1) of this section which (by virtue of section 69(3) of this Act) varies or revokes a previous order under that subsection—

(a) the reference in subsection (2) of this section to the planning area which the Secretary of State proposes should be specified in the order shall be construed as a reference to the planning area as it would be if the variation were made or, as the case may be, to the planning area as it is before the revocation ; and

(b) the order may contain such transitional provisions (including provisions as to the expenses and membership of any existing or former children's regional planning committee for a planning area) as the Secretary of State thinks fit.

Regional plans for community homes.
36.—(1) The children's regional planning committee for a planning area (in this and the following section referred to as " the committee ") shall prepare and submit to the Secretary of State, in accordance with the following provisions of this section, a plan (in this Act referred to as a " regional plan ") for the provision and maintenance of homes, to be known as community homes, for the accommodation and maintenance of children in the care of the relevant authorities.

(2) The community homes for which provision may be made by a regional plan shall be—

(a) community homes provided by the relevant authorities ; and

(b) voluntary homes provided by voluntary organisations but in the management of each of which the plan proposes that a relevant authority should participate in accordance with an instrument of management.

(3) Where a regional plan makes provision for any such voluntary home as is referred to in paragraph (b) of subsection (2) of this section, the plan shall designate the home as either a controlled community home or an assisted community home, according as it is proposed in the plan that the management, equipment and maintenance of the home should be the responsibility of one of the relevant authorities or of the voluntary organisation by which the home is provided.

(4) Every regional plan shall contain proposals—

(a) with regard to the nature and purpose of each of the community homes for which the plan makes provision ; and

(b) for the provision of facilities for the observation of the physical and mental condition of children in the care of the relevant authorities and for the assessment of the most suitable accommodation and treatment for those children.

(5) Before including provision in a regional plan that a community home should be provided by any of the relevant authorities or that a voluntary home provided by a voluntary organisation should be designated as a controlled or assisted community home, the committee shall obtain the consent of the authority or voluntary organisation by which the home is or is to be provided and, in the case of a home which is to be designated as a controlled or assisted community home, the consent of the local authority which it· is proposed should be specified in the instrument of management for the home.

(6) A regional plan shall be prepared in such form and shall contain such information as the Secretary of State may direct, either generally or in relation to a particular planning area or particular kinds of plans ; and the Secretary of State may direct that the· regional plan for a particular planning area shall be submitted to him within such period as may be specified in the direction or such longer period as he may allow.

37.—(1) After considering any regional plan submitted to him under section 36 of this Act and after making in the plan such modifications (if any) as he may agree with the committee by which the plan was submitted and as he may consider appropriate for securing that the plan makes proper provision for the accommodation and maintenance of children in the care of the relevant authorities,. the Secretary of State may approve the plan.

(2) Where the Secretary of State considers that, either with or without such modifications as are referred to in subsection (1) of this section, part but not the whole of a plan submitted to him under section 36 of this Act makes proper provision for the accommodation and maintenance of the children to whom that part of the plan relates, the Secretary of State may approve that part of the plan.

(3) Where the Secretary of State has approved part only of a regional plan, the committee for the planning area concerned shall prepare and submit to him under section 36 of this Act a further regional plan containing proposals to supplement that part of the previous plan which was approved by the Secretary of State.

(4) If, at any time after the approval of the whole or part of a regional plan by the Secretary of State, the committee for the planning area concerned consider that the plan, or such part of it as was approved should be varied or replaced, they shall prepare and submit to the Secretary of State under section

36 of this Act a further regional plan for that purpose ; and any such further regional plan may—

> (a) take the form of a replacement for the regional plan or part thereof which was previously approved by the Secretary of State ; or
>
> (b) contain proposals for the amendment of that regional plan or part thereof.

(5) In relation to a further regional plan which contains proposals for supplementing or amending a regional plan or part of a regional plan which has been previously approved by the Secretary of State (in this subsection referred to as " the approved plan ")—

> (a) section 36(4) of this Act shall have effect as if references to a regional plan were references to the approved plan as it would have effect if supplemented or amended in accordance with the proposals contained in the further regional plan ; and
>
> (b) subsection (1) of this section shall have effect as if the reference therein to children in the care of the relevant authorities were a reference to the children to whom the proposals in the plan relate ; and
>
> (c) in so far as the further regional plan contains proposals under which a home would cease to be a community home, or would become a community home of a different description, or would be used for a purpose different from that provided for in the approved plan, the committee preparing the further plan shall, before submitting it to the Secretary of State, obtain the consent of the local authority or voluntary organisation by which the home is provided and, if the proposal is for a home to become or to cease to be a controlled or assisted community home, the consent of the local authority which it is proposed should be, or which is, specified in the instrument of management for the home.

(6) Where the Secretary of State approves a regional plan, in whole or in part, he shall give notice in writing of his approval to the committee for the planning area concerned specifying the date on which the plan is to come into operation, and the committee shall send a copy of the notice to each of the relevant authorities and to any voluntary organisation whose consent was required to any provision of the plan.

Provision of community homes by local authorities. **38.** Where a regional plan for a planning area includes provision for a community home to be provided by one of the relevant authorities, it shall be the duty of the local authority concerned to provide, manage, equip and maintain that home.

39.—(1) The Secretary of State may by order make an instrument of management providing for the constitution of a body
of managers for any voluntary home which, in accordance with
a regional plan approved by him, is designated as a controlled
or assisted community home.

(2) Where in accordance with a regional plan approved by
the Secretary of State, two or more voluntary homes are designated as controlled community homes or as assisted community
homes, then if—

(a) those homes are, or are to be, provided by the same
voluntary organisation ; and

(b) the same local authority is to be represented on the
body of managers for those homes,

a single instrument of management may be made by the Secretary
of State under this section constituting one body of managers for
those homes or for any two or more of them.

(3) The number of persons who, in accordance with an instrument of management under this section, constitute the body of
managers for a voluntary home shall be such number, being
a multiple of three, as may be specified in the instrument of
management, but the instrument shall provide that a proportion
of the managers shall be appointed by such local authority as
may be so specified and—

(a) in the case of a voluntary home which is designated in
a regional plan as a controlled community home, the
proportion shall be two thirds ; and

(b) in the case of a voluntary home which is so designated
as an assisted community home, the proportion shall
be one-third.

(4) An instrument of management shall provide that the
" foundation managers ", that is to say, those of the managers
of the voluntary home to which the instrument relates who are
not appointed by a local authority in accordance with subsection (3) of this section, shall be appointed, in such manner and
by such persons as may be specified in the instrument,—

(a) so as to represent the interests of the voluntary organisation by which the home is, or is to be, provided ; and

(b) for the purpose of securing that, as far as practicable,
the character of the home as a voluntary home will
be preserved and that, subject to section 40(3) of this
Act, the terms of any trust deed relating to the home
are observed.

(5) An instrument of management under this section shall
come into force on such date as may be specified in the instrument, and if such an instrument is in force in relation to a

Part II

voluntary home the home shall be and be known as a controlled community home or an assisted community home, according to its designation in the regional plan.

Supplementary provisions as to instruments of management and trust deeds.

40.—(1) An instrument of management for a controlled or assisted community home shall contain such provisions as the Secretary of State considers appropriate for giving effect to the provisions of the regional plan by which the home is designated as a controlled or assisted community home, but nothing in the instrument of management for such a home shall affect the purposes for which the premises comprising the home are held.

(2) Without prejudice to the generality of subsection (1) of this section, an instrument of management may contain—

(a) provisions specifying the nature and purpose of the home or each of the homes to which it relates ;

(b) provisions requiring a specified number or proportion of the places in that home or those homes to be made available to local authorities and to any other body specified in the instrument ; and

(c) provisions relating to the management of that home or those homes and the charging of fees in respect of children placed therein or places made available to any local authority or other body.

(3) Subject to subsection (1) of this section, in the event of any inconsistency between the provisions of any trust deed and the instrument of management relating to a controlled or assisted community home, the instrument of management shall prevail over the provisions of the trust deed in so far as they relate to that home.

(4) After consultation with the voluntary organisation by which a controlled or assisted community home is provided and with the local authority specified in the instrument of management for the time being in force for that home, the Secretary of State may vary or revoke any provisions of that instrument of management by a further instrument of management.

(5) In this Act the expression " trust deed ", in relation to a voluntary home, means any instrument (other than an instrument of management) regulating the maintenance, management or conduct of the home or the constitution of a body of managers or trustees of the home.

Management of controlled community homes.

41.—(1) The management, equipment and maintenance of a controlled community home shall be the responsibility of the local authority specified in the instrument of management for that home, and in the following provisions of this section " the responsible authority ", in relation to such a home, means the local authority responsible for its management, equipment and maintenance.

(2) Subject to the following provisions of this section, the PART II responsible authority shall exercise their functions in relation to a controlled community home through the body of managers constituted by the instrument of management for the home, and any thing done, liability incurred or property acquired by the managers shall be done, incurred or acquired by the managers as agents of the responsible authority.

(3) In so far as any matter is reserved for the decision of the responsible authority, either by subsection (4) of this section or by the instrument of management for the controlled community home in question or by the service by the responsible authority on the managers or any of them of a notice reserving any matter, that matter shall be dealt with by the responsible authority themselves and not by the managers, but in dealing with any matter so reserved, the responsible authority shall have regard to any representations made to them by the managers.

(4) The employment of persons at a controlled community home shall be a matter reserved for the decision of the responsible authority, but where the instrument of management so provides the responsible authority may enter into arrangements with the voluntary organisation by which the home is provided whereby, in accordance with such terms as may be agreed between the responsible authority and the voluntary organisation, persons who are not in the employment of the responsible authority shall undertake duties at the home.

(5) The accounting year of the managers of a controlled community home shall be such as may be specified by the responsible authority and, before such date in each accounting year as may be so specified, the managers of a controlled community home shall submit to the responsible authority estimates, in such form as the authority may require, of expenditure and receipts in respect of the next accounting year ; and any expenses incurred by the managers of a controlled community home with the approval of the responsible authority shall be defrayed by that authority.

(6) The managers of a controlled community home shall keep proper accounts in respect of that home and proper records in relation to the accounts, but where an instrument of management relates to more than one controlled community home, one set of accounts and records may be kept in respect of all the homes to which the instrument relates.

42.—(1) The management, equipment and maintenance of Management an assisted community home shall be the responsibility of the of assisted voluntary organisation by which the home is provided, and community
homes. in the following provisions of this section " the responsible organisation ", in relation to such a home, means the voluntary organisation responsible for its management, equipment and maintenance.

(2) Subject to the following provisions of this section, the responsible organisation shall exercise its functions in relation to the home through the body of managers constituted by the instrument of management for the home, and any thing done, liability incurred or property acquired by the managers shall be done, incurred or acquired by the managers as agents of the responsible organisation.

(3) In so far as any matter is reserved for the decision of the responsible organisation, either by subsection (4) of this section or by the instrument of management for the assisted community home in question or by the service by the responsible organisation on the managers or any of them of a notice reserving any matter, that matter shall be dealt with by the responsible organisation itself and not by the managers, but in dealing with any matter so reserved the responsible organisation shall have regard to any representations made to the organisation by the managers.

(4) The employment of persons at an assisted community home shall be a matter reserved for the decision of the responsible organisation but, subject to subsection (5) of this section,—

(a) where the responsible organisation proposes to engage any person to work at the home or to terminate without notice the employment of any person at the home, the responsible organisation shall consult the local authority specified in the instrument of management and, if the local authority so directs, the responsible organisation shall not carry out its proposal without the consent of the local authority ; and

(b) the local authority may, after consultation with the responsible organisation, require the organisation to terminate the employment of any person at the home.

(5) Paragraphs (a) and (b) of subsection (4) of this section shall not apply—

(a) in such cases or circumstances as may be specified by notice in writing given by the local authority to the responsible organisation ; and

(b) in relation to the employment of any persons or class of persons specified in the instrument of management.

(6) The accounting year of the managers of an assisted community home shall be such as may be specified by the responsible organisation and, before such date in each accounting year as may be so specified, the managers of an assisted community home

shall submit to the responsible organisation estimates, in such form as the organisation may require, of expenditure and receipts in respect of the next financial year ; and all expenses incurred by the managers of an assisted community home with the approval of the responsible organisation shall be defrayed by the organisation.

(7) The managers of an assisted community home shall keep proper accounts in respect of that home and proper records in relation to those accounts, but where an instrument of management relates to more than one assisted community home, one set of accounts and records may be kept in respect of all the homes to which the instrument relates.

43.—(1) The Secretary of State may make regulations with respect to the conduct of community homes and for securing the welfare of the children in community homes.

(2) Without prejudice to the generality of subsection (1) of this section, regulations under this section may—

(a) impose requirements as to the accommodation and equipment to be provided in community homes and as to the medical arrangements to be made for protecting the health of the children in the homes ;

(b) impose requirements as to the facilities which are to be provided for giving religious instruction to children in community homes ;

(c) require the approval of the Secretary of State for the provision and use of accommodation for the purpose of restricting the liberty of children in community homes and impose other requirements as to the placing of a child in accommodation provided for that purpose, including a requirement to obtain the permission of the local authority or voluntary organisation in whose care the child is ;

(d) authorise the Secretary of State to give and revoke directions requiring the local authority by whom a community home is provided or who are specified in the instrument of management for a controlled community home or the voluntary organisation by which an assisted community home is provided to accommodate in the home a child in the care of a local authority for whom no places are made available in that home or to take such action in relation to a child accommodated in the home as may be specified in the directions ;

    (e) require reviews of any permission given in pursuance of paragraph (c) above and provide for such a review to be conducted in a manner approved by the Secretary of State by a committee of persons representing the local authority or voluntary organisation in question but including at least one person satisfying such conditions as may be prescribed by the regulations with a view to securing that he is independent of the authority or organisation and unconnected with any community home containing such accommodation as is mentioned in the said paragraph (c) ;

    (f) prescribe standards to which premises used for community homes are to conform ;

    (g) require the approval of the Secretary of State to the use of buildings for the purpose of community homes and to the doing of anything (whether by way of addition, diminution or alteration) which materially affects the buildings or grounds or other facilities or amenities available for children in community homes ;

    (h) provide that, to such extent as may be provided for in the regulations, the Secretary of State may direct that any provision of regulations under this section which is specified in the direction and makes any such provision as is referred to in paragraph (a), (f) or (g) above shall not apply in relation to a particular community home or the premises used for it, and may provide for the variation or revocation of any such direction by the Secretary of State.

(3) Without prejudice to the power to make regulations under this section conferring functions on the local authority or voluntary organisation by which a community home is provided or on the managers of a controlled or assisted community home, regulations under this section may confer functions in relation to a controlled or assisted community home on the local authority named in the instrument of management for the home.

(4) Where it appears to the Secretary of State that any premises used for the purposes of a community home are unsuitable for those purposes, or that the conduct of a community home is not in accordance with regulations made by him under this section or is otherwise unsatisfactory, he may by notice in writing served on the responsible body, direct that as from such date as may be specified in the notice the premises shall not be used for the purposes of a community home.

(5) Where the Secretary of State has given a direction in relation to a controlled or assisted community home under subsection (4) of this section and the direction has not been revoked.

the Secretary of State may at any time by order revoke the
instrument of management for that home.

(6) For the purposes of subsection (4) of this section the
responsible body—

(a) in relation to a community home provided by a local
authority, is that local authority ;

(b) in relation to a controlled community home, is the
local authority specified in the instrument of management for that home ; and

(c) in relation to an assisted community home, is the
voluntary organisation by which the home is provided.

44. While a voluntary home is a controlled or assisted com-   Controlled
munity home, the following enactments shall not apply in relation   and assisted
to it, that is to say,—   community
homes

(a) sections 29 and 30 of the Children Act 1948 (compul-   exempted from
sory registration of voluntary homes) ;   certain
provisions as

(b) section 31 of that Act (regulations as to conduct of   to voluntary
voluntary homes) ; and   homes.

(c) section 93 of the Act of 1933 and section 32 of the   1948 c. 43.
Children Act 1948 (notification to Secretary of State
of certain particulars relating to voluntary homes).

45.—(1) Subject to subsection (5) of this section, where any   Determination
dispute relating to a controlled community home arises between   of disputes
the local authority specified in the instrument of management   relating to
and either the voluntary organisation by which the home is   controlled
provided or any other local authority who have placed, or desire   and assisted
or are required to place, a child in their care in the home, the   community
dispute may be referred by either party to the Secretary of State   homes.
for his determination.

(2) Subject to subsection (5) of this section, where any dispute
relating to an assisted community home arises between the
voluntary organisation by which the home is provided and any
local authority who have placed, or desire to place, a child in
their care in the home, the dispute may be referred by either
party to the Secretary of State for his determination.

(3) Where a dispute is referred to the Secretary of State
under this section he may, in order to give effect to his determination of the dispute, give such directions as he thinks fit
to the local authority or voluntary organisation concerned.

(4) The provisions of this section shall apply notwithstanding
that the matter in dispute may be one which, under or by
virtue of the preceding provisions of this Part of this Act, is

Part II reserved for the decision, or is the responsibility, of the local authority specified in the instrument of management or, as the case may be, the voluntary organisation by which the home is provided.

(5) Where any trust deed relating to a controlled or assisted community home contains provision whereby a bishop or any other ecclesiastical or denominational authority has power to decide questions relating to religious instruction given in the home, no dispute which is capable of being dealt with in accordance with that provision shall be referred to the Secretary of State under this section.

Discontinuance of approved schools etc. on establishment of community homes.
1948 c. 58.

46.—(1) If in the case of any approved school, remand home, approved probation hostel or approved probation home within the meaning of the Criminal Justice Act 1948 (hereafter in this section referred to as an " approved institution ") it appears to the Secretary of State that in consequence of the establishment of community homes for a planning area the institution as such is no longer required, he may by order provide that it shall cease to be an approved institution on a date specified in the order.

(2) The provisions of Schedule 3 to this Act shall have effect in relation to institutions which are, or by virtue of this section have ceased to be, approved institutions.

Discontinuance by voluntary organisation of controlled or assisted community home.

47.—(1) The voluntary organisation by which a controlled or assisted community home is provided shall not cease to provide the home except after giving to the Secretary of State and the local authority specified in the instrument of management not less than two years' notice in writing of their intention to do so.

(2) A notice under subsection (1) of this section shall specify the date from which the voluntary organisation intends to cease to provide the home as a community home ; and where such a notice is given and is not withdrawn before the date specified in it, then, subject to subsection (4) of this section the instrument of management for the home shall cease to have effect on that date and accordingly the home shall then cease to be a controlled or assisted community home.

(3) Where a notice is given under subsection (1) of this section, the local authority to whom the notice is given shall inform the children's regional planning committee responsible for the regional plan under which the voluntary home in question was designated as a controlled or assisted community home of the receipt and content of the notice.

(4) Where a notice is given under subsection (1) of this section and the body of managers for the home to which the notice relates give notice in writing to the Secretary of State that they are unable or unwilling to continue as managers of the home until the date specified in the first-mentioned notice, the Secretary of State may by order—

(a) revoke the instrument of management ; and

(b) require the local authority who were specified in that instrument to conduct the home, until the date specified in the notice under subsection (1) of this section or such earlier date (if any) as may be specified for the purposes of this paragraph in the order, as if it were a community home provided by the local authority.

(5) Where the Secretary of State makes such a requirement as is specified in subsection (4)(b) of this section,—

(a) nothing in the trust deed for the home in question shall affect the conduct of the home by the local authority ; and

(b) the Secretary of State may by order direct that for the purposes of any provision specified in the direction and made by or under any enactment relating to community homes (other than this section) the home shall, until the date or earlier date specified as mentioned in subsection (4)(b) of this section, be treated as an assisted community home or as a controlled community home, but except in so far as the Secretary of State so directs, the home shall until that date be treated for the purposes of any such enactment as a community home provided by the local authority ; and

(c) on the date or earlier date specified as mentioned in subsection (4)(b) of this section the home shall cease to be a community home.

48.—(1) Where the instrument of management for a controlled or assisted community home ceases to have effect by virtue either of an order under section 43(5) of this Act or of subsection (2) or subsection (4)(a) of section 47 of this Act, the voluntary organisation by which the home was provided or, if the premises used for the purposes of the home are not vested in that organisation, the persons in whom those premises are vested (in this section referred to as " the trustees of the home "), shall become liable, in accordance with the following provisions of this section, to make repayment in respect of any increase in the value of the premises and other property belonging to the voluntary organisation or the trustees of the home which is attributable to the expenditure of public money thereon.

Financial provisions applicable on cessation of controlled or assisted community home.

(2) Where an instrument of management has ceased to have effect as mentioned in subsection (1) of this section and the instrument related—

    (*a*) to a controlled community home ; or

    (*b*) to an assisted community home which, at any time before that instrument of management came into force, was a controlled community home,

then, on the home ceasing to be a community home, the voluntary organisation by which the home was provided or, as the case may be, the trustees of the home, shall pay to the local authority specified in that instrument of management a sum equal to that part of the value of any relevant premises which is attributable to expenditure by the local authority who at the time the expenditure was incurred had responsibility for the management, equipment and maintenance of the home by virtue of section 41(1) of this Act.

(3) For the purposes of subsection (2) of this section, " relevant premises ", in relation to a controlled or assisted community home, means premises used for the purposes of the home and belonging to the voluntary organisation or the trustees of the home but erected, extended or improved, at any time while the home was a controlled community home, by the local authority having, at that time, such responsibility in relation to the home as is mentioned in subsection (2) of this section.

(4) Where an instrument of management has ceased to have effect as mentioned in subsection (1) of this section and the instrument related—

    (*a*) to an assisted community home ; or

    (*b*) to a controlled community home which, at any time before that instrument of management came into force, was an assisted community home,

then, on the home ceasing to be a community home, the voluntary organisation by which the home was provided or, as the case may be, the trustees of the home, shall pay to the Secretary of State a sum equal to that part of the value of the premises and any other property used for the purposes of the home which is attributable to the expenditure of money provided by way of grant under section 65 of this Act.

(5) Where an instrument of management has ceased to have effect as mentioned in subsection (1) of this section and the controlled or assisted community home to which it related was conducted in premises which formerly were used as an approved school or were an approved probation hostel or home but which were designated as a community home in a regional plan approved by the Secretary of State, then, on the home ceasing to be a community home, the voluntary organisation by which

the home was provided or, as the case may be, the trustees of　PART II
the home, shall pay to the Secretary of State a sum equal to
that part of the value of the premises concerned and of any
other property used for the purposes of the home and belonging
to the voluntary organisation or the trustees of the home which
is attributable to the expenditure—

> (a) of sums paid towards the expenses of the managers of
> an approved school under section 104 of the Act of
> 1933 ; or

> (b) of sums paid under section 77(3)(b) of the Criminal 1948 c. 58.
> Justice Act 1948 in relation to expenditure on approved
> probation hostels or homes.

(6) The amount of any sum payable under this section by
the voluntary organisation by which a controlled or assisted
community home was provided or by the trustees of the home
shall be determined in accordance with such arrangements—

> (a) as may be agreed between the voluntary organisation
> by which the home was provided and the local authority
> concerned or, as the case may be, the Secretary of
> State ; or

> (b) in default of agreement, as may be determined by the
> Secretary of State ;

and with the agreement of the local authority concerned or the
Secretary of State, as the case may be, the liability to pay any
sum under this section may be discharged, in whole or in part,
by the transfer of any premises or other property used for the
purposes of the home in question.

(7) The provisions of this section shall have effect notwithstanding anything in any trust deed for a controlled or assisted
community home and notwithstanding the provisions of any
enactment or instrument governing the disposition of the property
of a voluntary organisation.

(8) Any sums received by the Secretary of State under this
section shall be paid into the Consolidated Fund.

Consequential modifications of ss. 13 and 19 of
Children Act 1948

49. For section 13 of the Children Act 1948 there shall be Provision of
substituted the following section :—　　　　　　　　　　　accommoda-
　　　　　　　　　　　　　　　　　　　　　　　　　　　　tion and
Provision of　　**13.**—(1) A local authority shall discharge their maintenance
accommo-　　duty to provide accommodation and maintenance for children
dation and　　for a child in their care in such one of the following in care.
maintenance　ways as they think fit, namely,—　　　　　　　　　　1948 c. 43
for children
in care.　　　　　　(a) by boarding him out on such terms as to
　　　　　　　　　　　payment by the authority and otherwise as ·

PART II

the authority may, subject to the provisions of this Act and regulations thereunder, determine ; or

(b) by maintaining him in a community home or in any such home as is referred to in section 64 of the Children and Young Persons Act 1969 ; or

(c) by maintaining him in a voluntary home (other than a community home) the managers of which are willing to receive him ;

or by making such other arrangements as seem appropriate to the local authority.

(2) Without prejudice to the generality of sub-section (1) of this section, a local authority may allow a child in their care, either for a fixed period or until the local authority otherwise determine, to be under the charge and control of a parent, guardian, relative or friend.

(3) The terms, as to payment and other matters, on which a child may be accommodated and main-tained in any such home as is referred to in section 64 of that Act shall be such as the Secretary of State may from time to time determine.

Accommoda-tion of persons over school age in convenient community home.
1948 c. 43.

50. For section 19 of the Children Act 1948 there shall be substituted the following section:—

Accom-modation of persons over school age in convenient community home.

19. A local authority may provide accommoda-tion in a community home for any person who is over compulsory school age but has not attained the age of twenty-one if the community home is pro-vided for children who are over compulsory school age and is near the place where that person is employed or seeking employment or receiving educa-tion or training.

Foster children

Modification of general duty of local authorities with respect to foster children.
1958 c. 65.

51. For section 1 of the Children Act 1958 (which imposes a duty on every local authority to secure that foster children are visited by officers of the authority) there shall be substituted the following section:—

Duty of local authorities to ensure well-being of foster children

1. It shall be the duty of every local authority to satisfy themselves as to the well-being of children within their area who are foster children within the meaning of this Part of this Act and, for that pur-pose, to secure that, so far as appears to the authority to be appropriate, the children are visited from time to

time by officers of the authority and that such advice
is given as to the care and maintenance of the
children as appears to be needed.

52.—(1) In subsection (1 of section 2 of the Children Act
1958 (which, subject to the following provisions of that section,
defines a foster child for the purposes of Part I of that Act as a
child below the upper limit of the compulsory school age whose
care and maintenance are undertaken for reward for a period
exceeding one month by a person who is not a relative or
guardian of his) the words from " for reward " to " one month "
shall be omitted.

Amendments
of definitions
of " foster
child " and
" protected
child ".
1958 c. 65.

(2) At the end of paragraph (c) of subsection (3) of the said
section 2 (which provides that a child is not a foster child while
he is in the care of any person in a school) there shall be added
the words " in which he is receiving full time education ".

(3) After subsection (3) of the said section 2 there shall be
inserted the following subsection : —

(3A) A child is not a foster child within the meaning of
this Part of this Act at any time while his care and
maintenance are undertaken by a person, other than a
relative or guardian of his, if at that time—

(a) that person does not intend to, and does not in
fact, undertake his care and maintenance for a
continuous period of more than six days ; or

(b) that person is not a regular foster parent and does
not intend to, and does not in fact, undertake his
care and maintenance for a continuous period of
more than twenty-seven days ;

and for the purposes of this subsection a person is a regular
foster parent if, during the period of twelve months immediately preceding the date on which he begins to undertake the care and maintenance of the child in question, he
had, otherwise than as a relative or guardian, the care and
maintenance of one or more children either for a period of,
or periods amounting in the aggregate to, not less than
three months or for at least three continuous periods each
of which was of more than six days.

(4) Section 37 of the Adoption Act 1958 (which defines
" protected child " for the purposes of Part IV of that Act) shall
have effect subject to the following modifications : —

(a) in paragraph (a) of subsection (1) (which refers to
arrangements for placing a child in the care of a

person who is not a parent, guardian or relative of his) after the words "relative of his" there shall be inserted the words " but who proposes to adopt him " ;

(*b*) in subsection (1) (which among other matters excludes a foster child from the definition of "a protected child ") the words " but is not a foster child within the meaning of Part I of the Children Act 1958 " shall be omitted ; and

(*c*) in subsection (2) (which excludes certain children from the definition of protected child, including children only temporarily in the care and possession of a person under such arrangements as are referred to in sub-section (1)(*a*) of that section) the words from " by reason " to " that subsection, nor " shall be omitted.

(5) In consequence of the modifications of the definition of " protected child " specified in subsection (4) of this section, after subsection (4) of section 2 of the Children Act 1958 there shall be inserted the following subsection : —

1958 c. 65.

" (4A) A child is not a foster child for the purposes of this Part of this Act while he is placed in the care and possession of a person who proposes to adopt him under arrangements made by such a local authority or registered adoption society as is referred to in Part II of the Adoption Act 1958 or while he is a protected child within the meaning of Part IV of that Act."

1958 c. 5. (7 & 8 Eliz. 2.)

Modification of duty of persons maintaining foster children to notify local authority.

53.—(1) Section 3 of the Children Act 1958 (which requires any person maintaining foster children to notify the local authority on each occasion on which he receives a foster child) shall have effect subject to the following provisions of this section.

(2) In subsection (1) of the section (which requires at least two weeks advance notice of, or, in an emergency, notice within one week after, the reception of a foster child) at the beginning there shall be inserted the words " Subject to the following provisions of this section ", after the words " two weeks " there shall be inserted the words " and not more than four weeks " and for the words " one week " there shall be substituted the words " forty-eight hours ".

(3) In subsection (2) of the section (which relates to the content of the notice) after the word " specify " there shall be inserted the words " the date on which it is intended that the child should be received or, as the case may be, on which the child was in fact received or became a foster child and ".

(4) After subsection (2) of the section there shall be inserted the following subsection :—

(2A) A person shall not be required to give notice under subsection (1) of this section in relation to a child if—

    (*a*) he has on a previous occasion given notice under that subsection in respect of that or any other child, specifying the premises at which he proposes to keep the child in question ; and

    (*b*) he has not, at any time since that notice was given, ceased to maintain at least one foster child at those premises and been required by virtue of the following provisions of this section to give notice under subsection (5A) of this section in respect of those premises.

(5) In subsection (3) of the section (which relates to notification of changes of address of foster parents and requires similar periods of notice as under subsection (1))—

    (*a*) for the words " a foster child " there shall be substituted the words " one or more foster children " ;

    (*b*) for the words " the child is kept " there shall be substituted the words " the child is, or the children are, kept " ;

    (*c*) after the words " two weeks " there shall be inserted the words " and not more than four weeks " ; and

    (*d*) for the words " one week " there shall be substituted the words " forty-eight hours ".

(6) So much of subsection (4) of the section as requires notification that a foster child has been removed or has removed himself from the care of the person maintaining him shall cease to have effect and, accordingly, in that subsection for the words " that person " there shall be substituted the words " the person who was maintaining him " and in subsection (5) of the section (which dispenses with the need for such a notice where a child ceases to be a foster child on his removal from a foster parent but empowers the local authority concerned to require certain particulars in such a case)—

    (*a*) for the words " ceases to be a foster child on his removal " there shall be substituted the words " is removed or removes himself " ;

    (*b*) the words " need not give notice under subsection (4) of this section but " shall be omitted ; and

    (*c*) for the words from " the same " onwards there shall be substituted the words " the name and address, if known, of the person (if any) into whose care the child has been removed ".

C

(7) After subsection (5) of the section there shall be inserted the following subsections:—

(5A) Subject to the provisions of the following subsection, where a person who has been maintaining one or more foster children at any premises ceases to maintain foster children at those premises and the circumstances are such that no notice is required to be given under subsection (3) or subsection (4) of this section, that person shall, within forty-eight hours after he ceases to maintain any foster child at those premises, give notice in writing thereof to the local authority.

(5B) A person need not give the notice required by the preceding subsection in consequence of his ceasing to maintain foster children at any premises if, at the time he so ceases, he intends within twenty-seven days again to maintain any of them as a foster child at those premises; but if he subsequently abandons that intention or the said period expires without his having given effect to it he shall give the said notice within forty-eight hours of that event.

Inspection of premises in which foster children are kept.
1958 c. 65.

54.—(1) In section 4(1) of the Children Act 1958 (which empowers an officer of a local authority to inspect premises in the local authority's area in which foster children are being kept) after the word " in " in the second place where it occurs there shall be inserted the words " the whole or any part of ".

(2) After the said section 4(1) there shall be inserted the following subsection:—

(1A) If it is shown to the satisfaction of a justice of the peace on sworn information in writing—

(a) that there is reasonable cause to believe that a foster child is being kept in any premises, or in any part thereof, and

(b) that admission to those premises or that part thereof has been refused to a duly authorised officer of the local authority or that such a refusal is apprehended or that the occupier is temporarily absent,

the justice may by warrant under his hand authorise an officer of the local authority to enter the premises, if need be by force, at any reasonable time within forty-eight hours of the issue of the warrant, for the purpose of inspecting the premises.

(3) At the end of paragraph (b) of section 14(1) of the Children Act 1958 (which makes it an offence under that section to refuse to allow an inspection of any premises under section 4(1) of that Act) there shall be added the words " or wilfully

obstructs a person entitled to enter any premises by virtue of a   Part II
warrant under subsection (1A) of that section ".

55.—(1) In section 4(2) of the Children Act 1958 (which Imposition of
empowers a local authority to impose certain requirements on a requirements
person who keeps or proposes to keep foster children in premises and
used wholly or mainly for that purpose) for the word " mainly " prohibitions
there shall be substituted the word " partly ". relating to
the keeping
(2) After paragraph (*f*) of the said section 4(2) there shall be of foster
inserted the following paragraphs:— children.
1958 c. 65.
    (*g*) the fire precautions to be taken in the premises ;
    (*h*) the giving of particulars of any foster child received in
        the premises and of any change in the number or
        identity of the foster children kept therein.

(3) In the words following the several paragraphs of the said
section 4(2), after the word " but " there shall be inserted the
words " any such requirement may be limited to a particular
class of foster children kept in the premises and " and for the
words " (*b*) to (*f*) " there shall be substituted the words " (*b*) to
(*h*) ".

(4) For subsection (3) of section 4 of the Children Act 1958
(which empowers a local authority to prohibit a person from
keeping a particular foster child or any foster children at
particular premises) there shall be substituted the following subsections:—

    (3) Where a person proposes to keep a foster child in
any premises and the local authority are of the opinion
that—
        (*a*) the premises are not suitable premises in which
            to keep foster children ; or
        (*b*) that person is not a suitable person to have the
            care and maintenance of foster children ; or
        (*c*) it would be detrimental to that child to be kept
            by that person in those premises ;
the local authority may impose a prohibition on that
person under subsection (3A) of this section.

    (3A) A prohibition imposed on any person under this
subsection may—
        (*a*) prohibit him from keeping any foster child in
            premises specified in the prohibition ; or
        (*b*) prohibit him from keeping any foster child in any
            premises in the area of the local authority ; or
        (*c*) prohibit him from keeping a particular child
            specified in the prohibition in premises so
            specified.

(3B) Where a local authority have imposed a prohibition on any person under subsection (3A) of this section, the local authority may, if they think fit, cancel the prohibition, either of their own motion or on an application made by that person on the ground of a change in the circumstances in which a foster child would be kept by him.

1958 c. 65.

(5) In section 5(1) of the Children Act 1958 (which confers a right of appeal to a juvenile court within fourteen days of the imposition of a requirement or prohibition under section 4 of that Act) after the word " prohibition ", in the second place where it occurs, there shall be inserted the words " or, in the case of a prohibition imposed under subsection (3A) of that section, within fourteen days from the refusal by the local authority to accede to an application by him for the cancellation of the prohibition ".

Extension of disqualification for keeping foster children.

56.—(1) In section 6 of the Children Act 1958 (which provides that a person shall not, without the consent of the local authority, maintain a foster child if one or more of a variety of orders has been made against him) there shall be made the following amendments, that is to say—

(a) in paragraph (b), after the word " 1933 ", there shall be inserted the words " the Children and Young Persons Act 1969 " and for the words from " in respect of " to " of which the " there shall be substituted the words " and by virtue of the order or requirement a " ;

(b) at the end of paragraph (c) there shall be inserted the words " or has been placed on probation or discharged absolutely or conditionally for any such offence " ;

(c) in paragraph (e), after the word " subsection " there shall be inserted the words " (3) or " and for the words from " refusing " onwards there shall be substituted the words " refusing, or an order under section five of that Act cancelling, the registration of any premises occupied by him or his registration " ; and

(d) after paragraph (e) there shall be inserted the following paragraph : —

1958 c. 5. (7 & 8 Eliz. 2.)

(f) an order has been made under section 43 of the Adoption Act 1958 for the removal of a protected child who was being kept or was about to be received by him.

(2) At the end of the said section 6 there shall be added the following subsection : —

(2) Where this section applies to any person, otherwise than by virtue of this subsection, it shall apply also to any

other person who lives in the same premises as he does or who lives in premises at which he is employed ;

and accordingly the said section 6 as amended by the preceding subsection shall be subsection (1) of that section.

57.—(1) After subsection (1) of section 14 of the Children Act 1958 (which, among other matters, makes it an offence to maintain a foster child in contravention of section 6 of that Act) there shall be inserted the following subsection :—

(1A) Where section 6 of this Act applies to any person by virtue only of subsection (2) of that section, he shall not be guilty of an offence under paragraph (*d*) of subsection (1) of this section if he proves that he did not know, and had no reasonable ground for believing, that a person living or employed in the premises in which he lives was a person to whom that section applies.

(2) After subsection (2) of the said section 14 (which provides that offences under that section are punishable summarily) there shall be added the following subsection :—

(2A) If any person who is required, under any provision of this Part of this Act, to give a notice fails to give the notice within the time specified in that provision, then, notwithstanding anything in section 104 of the Magistrates' Courts Act 1952 (time limit for proceedings) proceedings for the offence may be brought at any time within six months from the date when evidence of the offence came to the knowledge of the local authority.

Inspection

58.—(1) Subject to subsection (2) of this section, the Secretary of State may cause to be inspected from time to time—

    (*a*) any community home provided by a local authority under section 38 of this Act ;

    (*b*) any voluntary home (whether a community home or not) ;

    (*c*) any other premises at which one or more children in the care of a local authority are being accommodated and maintained ;

    (*d*) any other premises at which one or more children are being boarded out by a voluntary organisation ; and

    (*e*) any other premises where a foster child within the meaning of Part I of the Children Act 1958 or a child to whom any of the provisions of that Part are extended by section 12 or section 13 of that Act, or a protected child within the meaning of Part IV of the Adoption Act 1958 is being accommodated or maintained.

(2) Subsection (1) of this section does not apply to any home or other premises which is, as a whole, subject to inspection by or under the authority of a government department.

(3) An inspection under this section shall be conducted by a person authorised in that behalf by the Secretary of State, but an officer of a local authority shall not be so authorised except with the consent of that authority.

(4) Any person inspecting a home or other premises under this section may inspect the children therein and make such examination into the state and management of the home or other premises and the treatment of children therein as he thinks fit.

Powers of entry supplemental to s. 58.

59.—(1) A person authorised to inspect any home or other premises under section 58 of this Act shall have a right to enter the home or other premises for that purpose and for any other purpose specified in subsection (4) of that section, but shall if so required produce some duly authenticated document showing his authority to exercise the power of entry conferred by this subsection.

(2) A person who obstructs the exercise by a person authorised as mentioned in subsection (1) of this section of a power of entry conferred thereby shall be liable on summary conviction to a fine not exceeding five pounds or, in the case of a second or subsequent conviction, to a fine not exceeding twenty pounds.

(3) A refusal to allow any such person as is mentioned in subsection (1) of this section to enter any such home or other premises as are mentioned in section 58(1) of this Act shall be deemed, for the purposes of section 40 of the Act of 1933 (which relates to search warrants), to be a reasonable cause to suspect that a child or young person in the home or other premises is being neglected in a manner likely to cause him unnecessary suffering or injury to health.

PART III

MISCELLANEOUS AND GENERAL

Miscellaneous

Extradition offences.

1870 c. 52.

60.—(1) There shall be included—

(*a*) in the list of extradition crimes contained in Schedule 1 to the Extradition Act 1870 ; and

(*b*) among the descriptions of offences set out in Schedule 1 to the Fugitive Offenders Act 1967, PART III
1967 c. 68.

any offence of the kind described in section 1 of the Act of 1933 (which relates to cruelty to persons under sixteen) and any offence of the kind described in section 1 of the Indecency with Children Act 1960. 1960 c. 33.

(2) Nothing in this Act shall be construed as derogating from the provisions of section 17 of the said Act of 1870 or section 16(2) or 17 of the said Act of 1967 in their application to any provisions of those Acts respectively as amended by the preceding subsection.

61.—(1) Without prejudice to the generality of the power to make rules under section 15 of the Justices of the Peace Act 1949 relating to the procedure and practice to be followed by magistrates' courts, provision may be made by such rules with respect to any of the following matters, namely,— Rules relating to juvenile court panels and composition of juvenile courts. 1949 c. 101.

(*a*) the formation and revision of juvenile court panels, that is to say, panels of justices specially qualified to deal with juvenile cases and the eligibility of justices to be members of such panels ;

(*b*) the appointment of persons as chairmen of juvenile courts ; and

(*c*) the composition of juvenile courts.

(2) Rules making any such provisions as are referred to in subsection (1) of this section may confer powers on the Lord Chancellor with respect to any of the matters specified in the rules and may, in particular, provide for the appointment of juvenile court panels by him and for the removal from a juvenile court panel of any justice who, in his opinion, is unsuitable to serve on a juvenile court.

(3) Rules made by virtue of this section may make different provision in relation to different areas for which juvenile court panels are formed ; and in the application of this section to the county palatine of Lancaster, for any reference in the preceding subsection to the Lord Chancellor there shall be substituted a reference to the Chancellor of the Duchy.

(4) Nothing in this section or in any rules made under section 15 of the said Act of 1949 shall affect—

(*a*) the areas for which juvenile court panels are formed and juvenile courts are constituted ,

(*b*) the provisions of Part I of Schedule 2 to the Act of 1963 (and, as it has effect by virtue of section 17(1) of that Act, Part I of Schedule 2 to the Act of 1933)

C 4

with respect to the making of recommendations and orders relating to the formation of combined juvenile court panels ; or

(c) the provisions of paragraph 14 of that Schedule relating to the divisions of the metropolitan area for which juvenile courts sit ;

but rules under the said section 15 may repeal, either generally or with respect to any part of the metropolitan area, any provision contained in paragraphs 15 to 18 of that Schedule (which contain provisions applicable in the metropolitan area with respect to certain of the matters referred to in subsection (1) of this section) and in subsections (2) and (3) of section 12 of the Administration of Justice Act 1964 (which amend those paragraphs).

1964 c. 42.

(5) In this section " the metropolitan area " means the inner London area and the City of London.

Contributions in respect of children and young persons in care.

62.—(1) The provisions of sections 86 to 88 of the Act of 1933 (which, as originally enacted, provided for contributions in respect of children and young persons committed to the care of a fit person or sent to an approved school) shall apply in relation to children and young persons committed to the care of a local authority by a care order which is not an interim order.

(2) Whether or not a contribution order has been made in respect of any child or young person in the care of a local authority, no contribution shall be payable in respect of him for any period during which he is allowed by the local authority to be under the charge and control of a parent, guardian, relative or friend, although remaining in the care of the local authority.

(3) Where a person (in this section referred to as a " contributory ") is liable under section 86 of the Act of 1933 to make a contribution in respect of a child or young person in the care of a local authority, then, subject to the following provisions of this section, the amount of his contribution shall be such as may be proposed by the local authority and agreed by the contributory or, in default of agreement, as may be determined by a court in proceedings for, or for the variation of, a contribution order.

(4) The maximum contribution which may be proposed by a local authority in respect of a child or young person in their care shall be a weekly amount equal to the weekly amount which, in the opinion of the local authority, they would normally be prepared to pay if a child or young person of the same age were boarded out by them (whether or not the child or young person in respect of whom the contribution is proposed is in fact so boarded out and, if he is, whether or not the local authority are in fact paying that amount).

(5) No contribution order shall be made on a contributory in respect of a child or young person unless—

   (a) the local authority in whose care he is have, by notice in writing given to the contributory, proposed an amount as the amount of his contribution ; and

   (b) either the contributory and the local authority have not, within the period of one month beginning with the day on which the notice was given to the contributory, agreed on the amount of his contribution or the contributory has defaulted in making one or more contributions of an amount which has been agreed.

(6) In proceedings for a contribution order, the court shall not order a contributory to pay a contribution greater than that proposed in the notice given to him under subsection (5)(a) of this section.

(7) In proceedings for the variation of a contribution order, the local authority concerned shall specify the weekly amount which, having regard to subsection (4) of this section, they propose should be the amount of the contribution and the court shall not vary the contribution order so as to require the contributory to pay a contribution greater than that proposed by the local authority.

(8) In this section—

   " contribution " means a contribution under section 86 of the Act of 1933 ; and

   " contribution order " means an order under section 87 of that Act.

63.—(1) Every local authority shall, at such times and in such form as the Secretary of State may direct, transmit to the Secretary of State such particulars as he may require—

   (a) with respect to the performance by the local authority of all or any of the functions specified in section 39(1) of the Children Act 1948 (which relates to the establishment of children's committees) ; and

   (b) with respect to the children in relation to whom the authority have exercised those functions.

Returns of information and presentation of reports etc. to Parliament. 1948 c. 43.

(2) Every voluntary organisation shall, at such times and in such form as the Secretary of State may direct, transmit to him such particulars as he may require with respect to the children who are accommodated and maintained in voluntary homes provided by the organisation or who have been boarded out by the organisation.

(3) The clerk of each juvenile court shall, at such times and in such form as the Secretary of State may direct, transmit to

PART III   him such particulars as he may require with respect to the proceedings of the court.

(4) The Secretary of State shall in each year lay before Parliament a consolidated and classified abstract of the information transmitted to him under the preceding provisions of this section.

1948 c. 43.   (5) The Secretary of State shall lay before Parliament in 1973 and in every third subsequent year a report with respect to the exercise by local authorities of the functions specified in section 39(1) of the Children Act 1948, the provision by voluntary organisations of facilities for children and such other matters relating to children as he thinks fit.

Financial provisions

Expenses of Secretary of State in providing homes offering specialised facilities.   **64.** There shall be defrayed out of moneys provided by Parliament any expenses incurred by the Secretary of State in providing, equipping and maintaining homes for the accommodation of children who are in the care of local authorities and are in need of particular facilities and services which are provided in those homes and are, in the opinion of the Secretary of State, unlikely to be readily available in community homes.

Grants to voluntary organisations etc.   **65.**—(1) The Secretary of State may make out of moneys provided by Parliament grants to voluntary organisations of such amounts and subject to such conditions as he may with the consent of the Treasury determine towards expenditure incurred by them in connection with the establishment, maintenance or improvement of voluntary homes which at the time the expenditure was incurred were assisted community homes or were designated as such in a regional plan which was then in operation, including expenses incurred by them in respect of the borrowing of money to defray any such expenditure.

(2) The power of the Secretary of State to make grants to voluntary organisations under section 46 of the Children Act 1948 (which relates to grants in respect of certain expenses incurred in connection with voluntary homes) shall not apply to expenditure incurred in connection with a voluntary home which, at the time the expenditure was incurred, was a controlled or assisted community home or was designated as such in a regional plan which was then in operation.

(3) Where an order has been made under section 46 of this Act in relation to an approved institution within the meaning of that section and no such provision as is referred to in paragraph 9(1) of Schedule 3 to this Act is made by a regional plan in relation to any part of the premises of the institution, the Secretary of State may with the consent of the Treasury

make out of moneys provided by Parliament grants towards the discharge by any person of any liability, other than an obligation to which paragraph 11 of that Schedule applies, which was incurred by that person in connection with the establishment, maintenance or improvement of the institution.

(4) No grant shall be made under subsection (3) of this section in respect of a liability relating to an institution unless it appears to the Secretary of State that, on or within a reasonable time after the date specified in the order referred to in that subsection, the premises of the institution are to be used for a purpose which is of benefit to children ; and any grant made under that subsection shall be subject to such conditions as the Secretary of State may with the approval of the Treasury determine, including conditions with respect to the repayment in whole or in part of the grant, either by the person to whom the grant was made or by some other person who, before the grant was made, consented to accept the liability.

(5) Any sums received by the Secretary of State by virtue of any such condition as is referred to in subsection (4) of this section shall be paid into the Consolidated Fund.

66.—(1) The power to make an order under section 3(1) of Increase of the Local Government Act 1966 increasing the amounts fixed rate support by a rate support grant order for a particular year shall be grants. exercisable, in accordance with subsection (2) of this section, in 1966 c. 42. relation to any rate support grant order made before the date of the coming into operation of any provision of this Act (in this section referred to as " the relevant provision ") for a grant period ending after that date.

(2) Without prejudice to subsection (4) of the said section 3 (which empowers an order under subsection (1) of that section to vary the matters prescribed by a rate support grant order), an order under subsection (1) of that section made by virtue of this section may be made for such year or years comprised in the grant period concerned as may be specified in the order and in respect of the year or each of the years so specified shall increase the amounts fixed by the relevant rate support grant order as the aggregate amounts of the rate support grants and any elements of the grants for that year to such extent and in such a manner as may appear to the Minister of Housing and Local Government to be appropriate, having regard to any additional expenditure incurred or likely to be incurred by local authorities in consequence of the coming into operation of the relevant provision.

(3) In this section " grant period " means the period for which a rate support grant order is made.

PART III   (4) There shall be defrayed out of moneys provided by Parliament any increase in rate support grants attributable to this Act.

Administrative
expenses.

67. Any administrative expenses of the Secretary of State under this Act shall be defrayed out of moneys provided by Parliament.

Supplemental

Compulsory
acquisition
of land.

68.—(1) A local authority other than a county council may be authorised by the Secretary of State to purchase compulsorily any land, whether situated inside or outside their area, for the purposes of their functions under this Act or section 1 of the Act of 1963.

1946 c. 49.

(2) The Acquisition of Land (Authorisation Procedure) Act 1946 shall apply in relation to the compulsory purchase of land in pursuance of subsection (1) of this section as if that subsection were contained in an Act in force immediately before the commencement of that Act.

1933 c. 51.

(3) In the application to the functions of a county council under this Act or section 1 of the Act of 1963 of section 159(1) of the Local Government Act 1933 (under which a county council may be authorised to purchase land compulsorily) the power to authorise a compulsory purchase shall be vested in the Secretary of State.

Orders and
regulations
etc.

69.—(1) Any power conferred on the Secretary of State by this Act to make an order or regulations, except an order under section 25, 39 or 43(5) or paragraph 23 or 24 of Schedule 4, shall be exercisable by statutory instrument; and any statutory instrument made in pursuance of this subsection, except an instrument containing only regulations under paragraph 8(2) of Schedule 3 or an order under section 1(6), 26, 46, 47, 72(2) or 73(2), or paragraph 11(2) of Schedule 3, shall be subject to annulment in pursuance of a resolution of either House of Parliament.

(2) A statutory instrument containing regulations under subsection (4) of section 5 or an order under section 34 of this Act shall not be subject to annulment as aforesaid, but no such regulations or order shall be included in a statutory instrument containing provisions which do not require approval in pursuance of the said subsection (4) or, as the case may be, to which subsection (7) of the said section 34 does not apply.

(3) An order made or directions given by the Secretary of State under any provision of this Act, except an order under section 7(5), may be revoked or varied by a subsequent order or subsequent directions under that provision.

(4) Any order or regulations made by the Secretary of State PART III
under this Act may—

(a) make different provision for different circumstances ;

(b) provide for exemptions from any provisions of the
order or regulations ; and

(c) contain such incidental and supplemental provisions as
the Secretary of State considers expedient for the purposes of the order or regulations.

70.—(1) In this Act, unless the contrary intention appears, the Interpretation
following expressions have the following meanings :— and ancillary
provisions.
"the Act of 1933" means the Children and Young Persons 1933 c. 12.
Act 1933 ;

"the Act of 1963" means the Children and Young Persons 1963 c. 37.
Act 1963 ;

"approved school order", "guardian" and "place of
safety" have the same meanings as in the Act of 1933 ;

"care order" has the meaning assigned to it by section 20
of this Act ;

"child", except in Part II (including Schedule 3) and
sections 27, 63, 64 and 65 of this Act, means a person
under the age of fourteen, and in that Part (including
that Schedule) and those sections means a person under
the age of eighteen and a person who has attained
the age of eighteen and is the subject of a care order ;

"instrument of management" means an instrument of
management made under section 39 of this Act ;

"interim order" has the meaning assigned to it by section
20 of this Act ;

"local authority" means the council of a county, county
borough or London borough or the Common Council
of the City of London ;

"petty sessions area" has the same meaning as in the
Magistrates' Courts Act 1952 except that, in relation 1952 c. 55.
to a juvenile court constituted for the metropolitan area
within the meaning of Part II of Schedule 2 to the Act
of 1963, it means such a division of that area as is
mentioned in paragraph 14 of that Schedule ;

"planning area" has the meaning assigned to it by section
35(1) of this Act ;

"police officer" means a member of a police force ;

"regional plan" has the meaning assigned to it by section
36(1) of this Act ;

PART III   " the relevant authorities ", in relation to a planning area,
                    has the meaning assigned to it by section 35(3) of this
                    Act ;
                " reside " means habitually reside, and cognate expressions
                    shall be construed accordingly except in section 12(4)
                    and (5) of this Act ;
                " supervision order ", " supervised person " and " super-
                    visor " have the meanings assigned to them by section
                    11 of this Act ;
                "trust deed ", in relation to a voluntary home, has the
                    meaning assigned to it by section 40(5) of this Act ;
                " voluntary home " has the same meaning as in Part V of
                    the Act of 1933 ;
                " voluntary organisation " has the same meaning as in the
1948 c. 43.   Children Act 1948 ; and
                " young person " means a person who has attained the age
                    of fourteen and is under the age of seventeen ;
            and it is hereby declared that, in the expression " care or
            control ", " care " includes protection and guidance and " con-
            trol " includes discipline.

            (2) Without prejudice to any power apart from this subsection
            to bring proceedings on behalf of another person, any power
            to make an application which is exercisable by a child or young
            person by virtue of section 15(1), 21(2), 22(4) or (6) or 28(5) of
            this Act shall also be exercisable on his behalf by his parent or
            guardian ; and in this subsection " guardian " includes any
            person who was a guardian of the child or young person in
            question at the time when any supervision order, care order or
            warrant to which the application relates was originally made.

            (3) In section 99(1) of the Act of 1933 (under which the
            age which a court presumes or declares to be the age of a
            person brought before it is deemed to be his true age for the
            purposes of that Act) the references to that Act shall be
            construed as including references to this Act.

            (4) Subject to the following subsection, any reference in this
            Act to any enactment is a reference to it as amended, and
            includes a reference to it as applied, by or under any other
            enactment including this Act.

            (5) Any reference in this Act to an enactment of the Parlia-
            ment of Northern Ireland shall be construed as a reference to
            that enactment as amended by any Act of that Parliament,
            whether passed before or after this Act, and to any enactment
            of that Parliament for the time being in force which re-enacts
            the said enactment with or without modifications.

71. This Act shall have effect, in its application to the Isles of Scilly, with such modifications as the Secretary of State may by order specify.

PART III
Application to I⋅⋅es of Scilly.

72.—(1) The transitional provisions and savings set out in Part I of Schedule 4 to this Act shall have effect.

(2) The transitional provisions set out in Part II of Schedule 4 to this Act shall have effect until such day as the Secretary of State may by order specify for the purposes of this subsection (being the day on and after which those provisions will in his opinion be unnecessary in consequence of the coming into force of provisions of the Social Work (Scotland) Act 1968) and shall be deemed to have been repealed on that day by an Act of Parliament passed after this Act.

(3) The enactments mentioned in Schedule 5 to this Act shall have effect subject to the amendments specified in that Schedule (which are minor amendments and amendments consequential on the provisions of this Act).

(4) Subject to subsection (1) of this section, the enactments mentioned in the first and second columns of Schedule 6 to this Act are hereby repealed to the extent specified in the third column of that Schedule.

(5) In accordance with Part II of this Act and the said Schedules 5 and 6, sections 1 to 6 and 14 of the Children Act 1958 are to have effect, after the coming into force of so much of that Part and those Schedules as relates to those sections, as set out in Schedule 7 to this Act, but without prejudice to any other enactment affecting the operation of those sections.

Transitional provisions, minor amendments and repeals etc.

1968 c. 49.

1958 c. 65.

73.—(1) This Act may be cited as the Children and Young Persons Act 1969, and this Act and the Children and Young Persons Acts 1933 to 1963 may be cited together as the Children and Young Persons Acts 1933 to 1969.

(2) This Act shall come into force on such day as the Secretary of State may by order appoint, and different days may be appointed under this subsection for different provisions of this Act or for different provisions of this Act so far as they apply to such cases only as may be specified in the order.

(3) Without prejudice to the generality of section 69(4) of this Act, an order under the preceding subsection may make such transitional provision as the Secretary of State considers appropriate in connection with the provisions brought into force by the order, including such adaptations of those provisions and of any other provisions of this Act then in force as appear to him appropriate for the purposes or in consequence of the operation of any

Citation, commencement and extent.

PART III
1968 c. 49.

provision of this Act before the coming into force of any other provision of this Act or of a provision of the Social Work (Scotland) Act 1968.

(4) This section and the following provisions only of this Act extend to Scotland, that is to say—

(a) sections 10(1) and (2), 32(1), (3) and (4), 56 and 57(1) ;

(b) section 72(2) and Part II of Schedule 4 ;

(c) paragraphs 25, 26, 33, 35, 38, 42, 43, 53, 54 and 57 to 83 of Schedule 5 and section 72(3) so far as it relates to those paragraphs ;

1894 c. 60.
1948 c. 33.
1965 c. 53.

(d) section 72(4) and Schedule 6 so far as they relate to the Merchant Shipping Act 1894, the Superannuation (Miscellaneous Provisions) Act 1948, sections 10, 53, 55 and 59 of the Act of 1963, the Family Allowances Act 1965 and the Social Work (Scotland) Act 1968.

(5) This section and the following provisions only of this Act extend to Northern Ireland, that is to say—

(a) sections 25 and 32 ;

1961 c. 39.

(b) section 72(3) and Schedule 5 so far as they relate to section 29 of the Criminal Justice Act 1961 and provisions of the Social Work (Scotland) Act 1968 which extend to Northern Ireland ; and

1937 c. 37.

(c) section 72(4) and Schedule 6 so far as they relate to section 83 of the Act of 1933, paragraph 13 of Schedule 2 to the Children and Young Persons (Scotland) Act 1937, section 29 of the Criminal Justice Act 1961, sections 10(1) and (2), 53(1) and 65(5) of, and paragraphs 27, 34 and 50 of Schedule 3 to, the Act of 1963 and sections 73(2), 76(1) and (2) and 77(1)(b) of the Social Work (Scotland) Act 1968 ;

1920 c. 67.

and section 32(2) and (3) of this Act shall be treated for the purposes of section 6 of the Government of Ireland Act 1920 as if it had been passed before the day appointed for the said section 6 to come into operation.

(6) Section 26 of this Act and this section, and section 72(4) of this Act and Schedule 6 to this Act so far as they relate to paragraph 13 of Schedule 2 to the Children and Young Persons (Scotland) Act 1937 and section 53(1) of, and paragraph 34 of Schedule 3 to, the Act of 1963, extend to the Channel Islands and the Isle of Man, and section 32(1) and (4) of this Act and this section extend to the Channel Islands.

(7) It is hereby declared that the provisions of sections 69 and 70 of this Act extend to each of the countries aforesaid so far as is appropriate for the purposes of any other provisions of this Act extending to the country in question.

SCHEDULES

SCHEDULE 1

MODIFICATIONS OF PART IV OF CRIMINAL JUSTICE ACT 1967

1.—(1) In section 73(1), after the word " proceedings " there shall be inserted the words " and the proceedings mentioned in subsections (3A) and (3B) of this section ".

(2) At the end of section 73(2) there shall be inserted the words " and any other magistrates' court to which the case is remitted in pursuance of section 56(1) of the Children and Young Persons Act 1933 ".

(3) In section 73, after subsection (3) there shall be inserted the following subsections : —

(3A) Where a person—

    (a) is or is to be brought before a juvenile court under section 1 of the Children and Young Persons Act 1969 ; or

    (b) is the subject of an application to a magistrates' court under section 15 or section 21 of that Act ; or

    (c) is or is to be brought before a juvenile court under section 31 of that Act,

the court may order that he shall be given legal aid for the purpose of proceedings before the court and, in a case falling within paragraph (a) of this subsection, before any juvenile court to which the case is remitted.

(3B) Where a person desires to appeal to a court of quarter sessions in pursuance of section 2(12), 3(8), 16(8), 21(4) or 31(6) of the said Act of 1969, that court or the court from whose decision the appeal lies may order that he be given legal aid for the purpose of the appeal.

2.—(1) At the end of section 74(2) there shall be inserted the words " and except in the case of proceedings under section 1 of the Children and Young Persons Act 1969 where it is alleged that the condition set out in subsection (2)(f) of that section is satisfied in consequence of an indictable offence and where the court is of the opinion aforesaid ".

(2) In section 74(3), after " (3) " there shall be inserted the word " (3B) " and for the word " either " there shall be substituted the word " any ".

(3) In section 74(5), after the word " (2) " there shall be inserted the words " or (3A) ".

(4) In section 74(6), after the word " section ", there shall be inserted the words " or to any person by a legal aid order under subsection (3B) of that section " and after the word " sentence " there shall be inserted the words " or, as the case may be dismissing the appeal mentioned in the said subsection (3B) or otherwise altering the order to which the appeal relates ".

SCH. 1

3. In section 75, after subsection (4) there shall be inserted the following subsection:—

(4A) Subsections (3) and (4) of this section shall have effect, in their application to a person who has not attained the age of sixteen, as if the words " he ", " him " and " his " referred to that person and a person who is an appropriate contributor in relation to him or such of them as the court selects, and as if for the word " shall " in subsection (4) there were substituted the word " may "; and the court may require that a statement furnished by an appropriate contributor in pursuance of subsection (4) shall specify both his means and those of the other person aforesaid.

4.—(1) In section 76, after subsection (1) there shall be inserted the following subsection:—

(1A) In a case where a legally assisted person has not attained the age of sixteen, the power conferred by the last foregoing subsection to order him to pay contributions in respect of the relevant costs shall include power to order any person who is an appropriate contributor in relation to him to pay such contributions; and for the purposes of any order proposed to be made by virtue of this subsection in connection with a legal aid order, an appropriate contributor who has failed to furnish a statement which he was required to furnish in pursuance of section 75(4) of this Act in connection with the legal aid order shall be deemed to have resources and commitments which are such that he may reasonably be ordered to pay the whole amount of the costs in question.

(2) In section 76(4)(*a*), after the words " that magistrates' court " there shall be inserted the words ", or any other magistrates' court to which the case is remitted in pursuance of section 56(1) of the Children and Young Persons Act 1933."

1933 c. 12.

(3) At the end of section 76 there shall be inserted the following subsection:—

(5) Nothing in subsection (4) of this subsection applies in a case where the legal aid order in question was made by virtue of section 73(3A) or (3B) of this Act, and in such a case an order under this section may be made—

(*a*) where the legal aid was ordered to be given for the purpose of proceedings before a magistrates' court, by that court, or any other magistrates' court to which the case is remitted in pursuance of section 2(11) of the Children and Young Persons Act 1969, after disposing of the case; and

(*b*) where the legal aid was ordered to be given for the purposes of an appeal to a court of quarter sessions, by that court after disposing of the appeal.

5. In section 77(1), after the words " assisted person ", there shall be inserted the words ", or a person who is an appropriate contributor in relation to him,", for the words " into his means " there

shall be substituted the words " into the means of that person and
any such contributor or of either or any of them " and the words
" on his means " shall be omitted.

6. In section 78(1), after the words " that he " there shall be
inserted the words " or any other person ".

7.—(1) In section 79(2), after the word " by " there shall be
inserted the words " or in respect of ", and for the words " to
him " there shall be substituted the words—

" (*a*) where the contribution was made by one person only, to
him ; and

(*b*) where the contribution was made by two or more persons,
to them in proportion to the amounts contributed by them ".

(2) In section 79(3) and section 79(6) after the words " assisted
person " there shall be inserted the words " or an appropriate
contributor ".

8.—(1) In section 84, in the definition of " appropriate authority ",
after paragraph (*a*) there shall be inserted the following paragraph : —

(*aa*) in relation to legal aid ordered by virtue of section 73(3A)
or (3B) of this Act, the clerk of the magistrates' court before
which the proceedings were heard or from which the appeal
was brought or the clerk of the magistrates' court nominated
for the purposes of this paragraph by the first-mentioned
court.

(2) In section 84, after the definition aforesaid there shall be
inserted the following : —

" appropriate contributor ", in relation to a person who has not
attained the age of sixteen, means his father, any person
who has been adjudged to be his putative father and
(whether or not he is legitimate) his mother.

(3) At the end of section 84 there shall be inserted the following
subsections : —

(2) Any power to make an application in pursuance of this
Part of this Act which is exercisable by a person who has not
attained the age of seventeen shall also be exercisable by his
parent or guardian on his behalf, without prejudice to any
powers of the parent or guardian apart from this subsection ;
and in this subsection " guardian " has the same meaning as in
section 70(2) of the Children and Young Persons Act 1969.

(3) A person who attains the age of sixteen after a legal aid
order is made in respect of him or, in a case where such an
order is made in pursuance of an application, after the application is made, shall be treated for the purposes of this Part
of this Act, in relation to the order, as not having attained that
age.

and accordingly the said section 84 as amended by sub-paragraphs
(1) and (2) of this paragraph shall be subsection (1) of that section.

Section 35(4)

SCHEDULE 2

CHILDREN'S REGIONAL PLANNING COMMITTEES

1.—(1) Subject to the following provisions of this Schedule, the children's regional planning committee for a planning area (in this Schedule referred to as "the committee") shall consist of such number of persons selected and appointed in such manner and holding office on such terms as the relevant authorities may from time to time approve.

1933 c. 51.

(2) No person who is disqualified by virtue of section 59 of the Local Government Act 1933 from being a member of any local authority which is one of the relevant authorities for a planning area may be a member of the committee for that area.

2.—(1) Subject to sub-paragraph (2) of this paragraph, the relevant authorities for a planning area shall so exercise their powers under paragraph 1(1) of this Schedule as to secure that each authority nominates as a member of the committee for the area at least one person who is not so nominated by any other of the revelant authorities.

(2) If the Secretary of State considers that owing to special circumstances the requirement imposed by sub-paragraph (1) of this paragraph should be dispensed with in the case of a particular authority he may direct accordingly.

(3) The members of the committee for a planning area who are nominated by the relevant authorities are in the following provisions of this Schedule referred to as " the nominated members ".

3.—(1) Without prejudice to any power of co-option conferred on the committee for a planning area under paragraph 1(1) of this Schedule, but subject to paragraph 4 of this Schedule, the nominated members of the committee may co-opt other persons to serve as members of the committee, either generally or in relation only to such matters as may be specified by the nominated members.

(2) Where any persons are co-opted to serve as members of the committee for a planning area in relation only to such matters as are specified by the nominated members then, subject to any directions given by the relevant authorities, the extent to which those persons shall be entitled to attend, speak and vote at meetings of the committee shall be such as may be determined by the nominated members.

4. The relevant authorities for a planning area shall so exercise their powers under paragraph 1(1) of this Schedule, and the nominated members of the committee for a planning area shall so limit any exercise of their power under paragraph 3 of this Schedule, as to secure that at all times a majority of the members of the committee for the planning area are members of the relevant authorities.

5. Subject to any directions given by the relevant authorities, the procedure and quorum of the committee for a planning area shall be such as may be determined by the nominated members.

6. Section 93(1) of the Local Government Act 1933 (which relates to the expenses of joint committees of local authorities) shall apply to the committee for a planning area as it applies to such a joint committee as is mentioned in that section, but as if—

    (a) for references to the local authorities by whom the committee is appointed there were substituted references to the relevant authorities ; and

    (b) for paragraphs (a) and (b) of subsection (1) of that section there were substituted the words " by the Secretary of State " ;

and Part X of that Act (which relates to accounts and audit) shall apply to the accounts of the committee for a planning area as it applies to the accounts of such a joint committee as is mentioned in section 219(c) of that Act.

SCHEDULE 3

APPROVED SCHOOLS AND OTHER INSTITUTIONS

Provisions as to staff

1.—(1) This paragraph applies where it appears to the Secretary of State that on the date specified in an order under section 46 of this Act (in the following provisions of this Schedule referred to as a " section 46 order ") all or any of the premises used for the purposes of the institution to which the order relates are to be used for the purposes—

    (a) of a community home, or

    (b) of a school of any of the following descriptions, namely, a county school, a voluntary school which is a controlled or aided school, or a special school ;

and in this Schedule " the specified date ", in relation to an institution to which a section 46 order relates, means the date specified in that order.

(2) Where this paragraph applies the Secretary of State may, by the section 46 order, make such provision as he considers appropriate with respect to—

    (a) the transfer of existing staff to the employment of the authority, voluntary organisation or other body of persons responsible for the employment of persons at the community home or school, as the case may be ; and

    (b) the transfer to a local authority or voluntary organisation specified in the order of any liabilities (including contingent and future liabilities) with respect to the payment of superannuation and other benefits to or in respect of existing staff and retired staff.

(3) If any such superannuation or other benefits as are referred to in sub-paragraph (2)(b) of this paragraph are not benefits to which the Pensions (Increase) Acts 1920 to 1969 or any of those Acts apply, the

section 46 order may contain such provisions as the Secretary of State considers appropriate—

    (a) for securing the continued payment of additional amounts (calculated by reference to increases under those Acts) which were paid before the specified date in respect of any such benefits ; and

    (b) for securing the payment of additional amounts (calculated by reference to increases under those Acts) in respect of any such benefits to which any person became entitled before the specified date but in respect of which no similar additional amounts were paid before that date.

(4) Where this paragraph applies the section 46 order—

    (a) shall contain provisions for the protection of the interests of any existing staff whose employment is transferred as mentioned in sub-paragraph (2)(a) of this paragraph ;

    (b) may contain provisions for the protection of the interests of existing staff whose employment is not so transferred ; and

    (c) may contain provisions applying, amending or repealing any provision made by or under any enactment and relating to the conditions of service of existing staff or the payment of superannuation and other benefits to or in respect of existing or retired staff ;

and in a case falling within sub-paragraph (1)(b) of this paragraph any provisions made under paragraph (a) of this sub-paragraph shall have effect notwithstanding any provision made by or under any enactment and relating to the remuneration of teachers.

(5) In this paragraph " existing staff " in relation to a section 46 order means persons who, immediately before the specified date, were employed for the purposes of the institution to which the order relates, and " retired staff " in relation to such an order means persons who, at some time before the specified date, were employed for those purposes but ceased to be so employed before the specified date.

2.—(1) Regulations under section 60 of the Local Government Act 1958 may make provision in relation to persons who suffer loss of employment or loss or diminution of emoluments as a result of a section 46 order and, if in such a case the Minister by whom the regulations are made thinks fit, the regulations may provide for the payment of compensation by the Secretary of State instead of by an authority prescribed by or determined under the regulations.

(2) In accordance with sub-paragraph (1) of this paragraph, sub-section (2) of the said section 60 shall be amended as follows :

    (a) after the words " under the regulations " there shall be inserted the words " or, in a case to which paragraph 2 of Schedule 3 to the Children and Young Persons Act 1969 applies, by the Secretary of State " ; and

    (b) after the words " order under Part I of the Police Act 1964 " there shall be inserted the words " or of an order under section 46 of the Children and Young Persons Act 1969 ".

(3) Where a section 46 order is made in relation to an approved   Sᴄʜ. 3
institution but paragraph 1 of this Schedule does not apply in relation
to that institution, the section 46 order may make such provision as
the Secretary of State considers appropriate with respect to the transfer to him of any such liabilities as are referred to in sub-paragraph
(2)(*b*) of that paragraph and the payment by him of any such
additional amount as is referred to in sub-paragraph (3) of that
paragraph.

Use of premises as homes for children in care

3.—(1) If on the day specified for the purposes of section 7(5) of
this Act premises are used for the purposes of an approved school,
then during the period (in this Schedule referred to, in relation to an
approved school, as " the interim period ") beginning immediately
after that day and ending on the day on which the school ceases to
be an approved school (whether by virtue of a section 46 order or
otherwise) those premises may be used for the accommodation and
maintenance of children in the care of local authorities.

(2) If during the interim period the premises of an approved
school are used for the accommodation and maintenance of children
in the care of a local authority then, during that period,

   (*a*) any reference in section 21(1) or section 31 of this Act to a
        community home includes a reference to those premises ;
        and

   (*b*) for the reference in section 18(1)(*c*) of the Criminal Justice 1961 c. 39.
        Act 1961 (directions of Secretary of State as to management
        of approved schools) to persons under the care of the
        managers there shall be substituted a reference to the
        children in the care of local authorities who are accom-
        modated and maintained in those premises.

(3) At the request of the managers of an approved school the
Secretary of State may, at any time during the interim period,
give a direction—

   (*a*) that so much as may be specified in the direction of any
        rules made under paragraph 1(1) of Schedule 4 to the
        Act of 1933 (approved school rules) and of any rules
        made by the managers and approved by him under
        paragraph 1(2) of that Schedule shall no longer apply in
        relation to that school ; and

   (*b*) that, in place of those rules, so much as may be speci-
        fied in the direction of any regulations made under section
        43 of this Act shall apply, subject to such adaptations
        and modifications as may be so specified, in relation to
        the approved school as if it were a community home.

(4) If the effect of the application, by a direction under sub-
paragraph (3) above, of any provision of regulations made under
section 43 of this Act in relation to an approved school would be to
impose any duty or confer any power on a local authority in
relation to that school, the Secretary of State shall not give a
direction applying that provision except with the consent of the local
authority concerned.

SCH. 3   4.—(1) If on the day specified for the purposes of section 7(5) of this Act a remand home was designated under section 11 of the Act of 1963 as a classifying centre then, during the period beginning immediately after that day and ending on the date specified in a section 46 order relating to that home, the home may be used for the accommodation and maintenance of children in the care of local authorities.

(2) In this Schedule " classifying centre " means a remand home designated as mentioned in sub-paragraph (1) of this paragraph and, in relation to a classifying centre, the period specified in that sub-paragraph is referred to as " the interim period ".

(3) During the interim period—

    (a) the expenses of a local authority in providing and maintaining a classifying centre in relation to the whole or part of the expenses of which a direction has been given by the Secretary of State under section 11(3) of the Act of 1963 shall be treated for the purposes of section 104 of the Act of 1933 as if they were expenses incurred by the authority as managers of an approved school ;

    (b) subsections (4) and (5) of section 106 of the Act of 1933 shall apply in relation to a classifying centre as they apply in relation to an approved school the managers of which are a local authority ; and

    (c) any reference in section 21(1) or section 31 of this Act to a community home includes a reference to a classifying centre.

5.—(1) Where a section 46 order is made in relation to an approved school or approved probation hostel or home and, in a regional plan approved by the Secretary of State, the whole or any part of the premises of the institution is designated as a controlled or assisted community home, the premises so designated may, after the specified date, be used for the purpose specified in the regional plan.

(2) Without prejudice to any power to vary the provisions of a trust deed relating to a community home consisting of premises designated as mentioned in sub-paragraph (1) of this paragraph, the purpose referred to in that sub-paragraph shall be deemed to be included among the purposes for which the premises are held in accordance with a trust deed relating to that home.

6.—(1) Where a section 46 order is made in relation to an approved institution (other than an institution provided by a local authority) and, in a regional plan approved by the Secretary of State, the whole or any part of the premises of the institution is designated as a community home to be provided by a local authority, then if the Secretary of State is satisfied that the premises so designated were to a substantial extent provided with the assistance of grants under section 104 of the Act of 1933 or section 77 of the Criminal Justice Act 1948, he may, by an authorisation in writing under this paragraph, authorise the transfer of the premises so designated to that local authority.

1948 c. 58,

(2) The transfer of any premises in pursuance of an authorisation under this paragraph—

(a) shall be on such terms, as to payment and other matters, as may be agreed between the local authority concerned and the trustees or other persons in whom the premises are vested and, if the authorisation so provides, as may be approved by the Secretary of State ;

(b) shall not take effect before the specified date ; and

(c) shall operate to vest the premises transferred in the local authority free from any charitable trust and from any other obligation requiring the use of the premises for the purposes of an approved institution.

(3) Before giving an authorisation under this paragraph authorising the transfer of any premises belonging to a charity or otherwise held on charitable trusts, the Secretary of State shall consult the Charity Commissioners.

7. The provisions of paragraphs 3 to 6 of this Schedule shall have effect notwithstanding anything in the law relating to charities or in any deed or other instrument regulating the purposes for which any premises may be used.

Financial provisions

8.—(1) During the period which is the interim period in relation to an approved school or to a classifying centre falling within paragraph 4(3)(a) of this Schedule contributions shall be payable by local authorities to the managers of that school or, as the case may be, the local authority providing the classifying centre in respect of children in the care of the authorities who are accommodated and maintained in the school premises or the classifying centre in accordance with paragraph 3(1) or paragraph 4(1) of this Schedule.

(2) The contributions payable by a local authority under sub-paragraph (1) above in respect of a child in their care shall be payable throughout the time during which the child is accommodated and maintained in the approved school or classifying centre concerned and shall be such as may be prescribed by regulations made by the Secretary of State.

9.—(1) Where a section 46 order is made in relation to an approved institution, other than an institution provided by a local authority, and in a regional plan approved by the Secretary of State the whole or any part of the premises of the approved institution is designated as a community home, then,—

(a) on the coming into force of an instrument of management for a voluntary home which consists of or includes the premises so designated ; or

(b) on the transfer of the premises so designated to a local authority in pursuance of an authorisation under paragraph 6 of this Schedule,

any such obligation relating to that institution as is referred to in sub-paragraph (2) of this paragraph shall cease.

SCH. 3

(2) Sub-paragraph (1) of this paragraph applies to any obligation arising by virtue of a condition imposed under either of the following enactments, namely,—

(*a*) section 104 of the Act of 1933 (expenses of managers of an approved school) ; or

1948 c. 58.

(*b*) section 77 of the Criminal Justice Act 1948 (expenditure in connection with approved probation hostels or homes).

(3) In a case falling within sub-paragraph (1) of this paragraph, the section 46 order may contain provisions requiring the responsible authority or organisation or, as the case may be, the local authority to whom the premises are transferred, to pay to the Secretary of State such sum as he may determine in accordance with sub-paragraph (4) of this paragraph by way of repayment of a proportion of any grants made in relation to the former approved institution under either of the enactments referred to in sub-paragraph (2) of this paragraph, but where the community home concerned is an assisted community home, the section 46 order may provide that, with the consent of the Treasury, the Secretary of State may reduce the sum to be paid to him in accordance with the preceding provisions of this sub-paragraph to such sum as he thinks fit.

(4) For the purpose of determining any such sum as is mentioned in sub-paragraph (3) of this paragraph, the Secretary of State shall assess—

(*a*) the amount which in his opinion represents the proportion of the total amount of the grants paid in respect of expenditure in connection with the former approved institution which was attributable to expenditure of a capital nature ; and

(*b*) the amount which in his opinion represents the proportion of the contributions paid by local authorities under section 90 of the Act of 1933 or, as the case may be, the proportion of the sums paid by probation committees under rules made under Schedule 5 to the Criminal Justice Act 1948 which (in either case) should be treated as having been paid on account of expenditure of a capital nature in connection with the former approved institution ;

and the sum determined by the Secretary of State for the purpose of sub-paragraph (3) of this paragraph shall be equal to the amount by which the amount assessed under paragraph (*a*) above exceeds twice the amount assessed under paragraph (*b*) above.

(5) If the instrument of management for an assisted community home ceases to have effect as mentioned in subsection (1) of section 48 of this Act there shall be deducted from any sum which is payable to the Secretary of State under subsection (5) of that section any sums paid to him by the responsible organisation in respect of the assisted community home in pursuance of any such provisions of a section 46 order relating to the former approved institution as are referred to in sub-paragraph (3) of this paragraph.

(6) In this paragraph "the former approved institution", in relation to a community home, means the approved institution the whole or part of the premises of which are comprised in that home.

10.—(1) The provisions of this paragraph apply where in a regional plan approved by the Secretary of State, the whole or any part of the premises of an approved institution to which a section 46 order relates is designated as a controlled or assisted community home and an instrument of management for a community home which consists of or includes the premises so designated has come into force ; and in this paragraph "the former approved institution", in relation to such a community home, means the approved institution the whole or part of the premises of which are comprised in that home.

(2) Where this paragraph applies and the community home concerned is a controlled community home, then—

   (a) the Secretary of State may, by the section 46 order, make such provision as he considers appropriate for the transfer to the responsible authority of any rights, liabilities and obligations which, immediately before the specified date, were rights, liabilities and obligations of the managers of, or the society or person carrying on, the former approved institution ; and

   (b) except in so far as the section 46 order otherwise provides, any legal proceedings pending immediately before the specified date by or against those managers or that society or person shall be continued on and after that date, with the substitution of the responsible authority for those managers or that society or person as a party to the proceedings.

(3) Where this paragraph applies and the community home concerned is an assisted community home but the responsible organisation does not consist of the persons who were the managers of or, as the case may be, is not the society or person who carried on, the former approved institution, paragraphs (a) and (b) of sub-paragraph (2) of this paragraph shall apply with the substitution for any reference to the responsible authority of a reference to the responsible organisation.

(4) If any liabilities of a voluntary organisation which is the responsible organisation in relation to an assisted community home falling within sub-paragraph (1) of this paragraph were incurred by the organisation before the specified date or were transferred to the organisation by the section 46 order (by virtue of sub-paragraph (3) of this paragraph) and, in either case, had the former approved institution continued to be an approved institution, any expenditure incurred in meeting those liabilities would have been eligible for a grant out of moneys provided by Parliament—

   (a) under section 104(1)(a) of the Act of 1933 as the expenses of the managers of an approved school, or

   (b) under section 77(3)(b) of the Criminal Justice Act 1948, as 1948 c. 58 expenditure falling within that section and relating to an approved probation hostel or home, then any expenditure incurred after the specified date by the responsible organisation in meeting those liabilities shall be deemed for the purposes of section 65(1) of this Act to be expenditure incurred by the responsible organisation in connection with the assisted community home in question.

11.—(1) Where a section 46 order is made in relation to an approved institution and no such provision as is referred to in sub-paragraph (1) of paragraph 9 of this Schedule is made by a regional plan in relation to any part of the premises of the institution, the person or persons on whom falls any such obligation (in this paragraph referred to as a " repayment obligation ") relating to the institution as is referred to in sub-paragraph (2) of that paragraph may apply to the Secretary of State for an order under this paragraph.

(2) If, on an application under sub-paragraph (1) of this paragraph, it appears to the Secretary of State that on or within a reasonable time after the specified date the premises of the institution concerned or the proceeds of sale of the whole or any part of those premises are to be used for a purpose which is of benefit to children, he may with the consent of the Treasury make an order—

(*a*) substituting for the conditions under which the repayment obligation arose such different conditions as he considers appropriate with respect to the repayment of any sum to which the repayment obligation relates ; and

(*b*) if the person or persons on whom the repayment obligation falls so request, imposing any liability to repay a sum in pursuance of the substituted conditions referred to in paragraph (*a*) above on such other person or persons as consent to accept the liability and as, in the opinion of the Secretary of State, will be able to discharge that liability.

Interpretation

12. In this Schedule—

" approved institution " has the same meaning as in section 46 of this Act ;

" the responsible authority ", in relation to a controlled community home, has the same meaning as in section 41 of this Act ;

" the responsible organisation ", in relation to an assisted community home, has the same meaning as in section 42 of this Act ; and

" section 46 order " and, in relation to an institution to which such an order relates, " specified date " have the meanings assigned to them by paragraph 1(1) of this Schedule.

SCHEDULE 4

TRANSITIONAL PROVISIONS AND SAVINGS

PART I

GENERAL

1. For the purposes of subsection (4) of section 1 and subsection (7) of section 7 of this Act, any order under the Act of 1933 committing a child or young person to the care of a fit person other than a local authority, any supervision order under that Act and any order to enter into recognisances in pursuance of section 62(1)(c) of that Act shall be deemed to be such an earlier order as is mentioned in those subsections.

2.—(1) Nothing in section 4 of this Act affects any proceedings against a person for an offence with which by virtue of that section he has ceased to be chargeable since the proceedings were begun ; but where a person is found guilty of an offence and by reason of that section could not have been charged with it on the date of finding, then, subject to sections 1(5) and 2(13) of this Act, the court may make an order under section 1 of this Act in respect of the offender or an order discharging him absolutely but shall not have power to make any other order in consequence of the finding.

(2) Nothing in section 4 of this Act shall be construed as preventing any act or omission which occurred outside the United Kingdom from being a civil offence for the purposes of the Army Act 1955, 1955 c. 18. the Air Force Act 1955, or the Naval Discipline Act 1957, or from 1955 c. 19. being dealt with under any of those Acts. 1957 c. 53.

3. Nothing in section 5 of this Act affects any information laid in respect of a person before the date on which apart from this paragraph the information would have been required by virtue of that section to contain a statement of his age.

4. Where a person is committed for trial by a jury before subsection (1) of section 6 of this Act comes into force, or claims to be tried by a jury before subsection (2) of that section comes into force, proceedings in respect of the offence in question shall not be affected by the coming into force of that subsection.

5.—(1) The coming into force of section 7(1) or of an order under section 34(1)(d) of this Act shall not affect any sentence of borstal training passed before the date when the said section 7(1) or the order came into force or any committal for sentence before that date under section 28(1) of the Magistrates' Courts Act 1952 ; 1952 c. 55. but a sentence of borstal training shall not be passed on any person (including a person to whom such a committal relates) if on the date of the relevant conviction he had not attained the minimum age which is for the time being specified in section 20(1) of the Criminal Justice Act 1948. 1948 c. 58.

(2) Nothing in section 7(2) of this Act affects a probation order made before the coming into force of the said section 7(2).

SCH. 4
1948 c. 58.

1961 c. 39.

6. No order shall be made under section 19(1) of the Criminal Justice Act 1948, at any time after the coming into force of this paragraph and before the coming into force of paragraph 23 of Schedule 5 to this Act, in respect of a person under the age of seventeen in consequence of a default within the meaning of the Criminal Justice Act 1961.

7.—(1) Every approved school order in force on the specified day shall cease to have effect at the end of that day ; and after that day—

> (a) no person shall be detained by virtue of section 73 or section 82 of the Act of 1933 or an order under paragraph 2 of Schedule 2 to the said Act of 1961 or be subject to supervision in pursuance of that Schedule ; and

> (b) no person who has attained the age of nineteen shall be detained by virtue of a warrant under section 15 of the said Act of 1961.

(2) A person who has not attained the age of nineteen on the specified day and who, but for sub-paragraph (1) of this paragraph, would after that day have been the subject of an approved school order or liable to be detained or subject to supervision as mentioned in that sub-paragraph shall be deemed from the end of that day—

> (a) to be the subject of a care order made by the court which made the approved school order in question on the same day as that order and committing him to the care of the local authority named in the approved school order in pursuance of section 70(2) of the Act of 1933 or, if no authority is so named, of a local authority nominated in relation to him by the Secretary of State ; and

> (b) in the case where he would have been subject to supervision as aforesaid, to have been allowed by the said local authority to be under the charge and control of the person last nominated in relation to him in pursuance of paragraph 1(1) of Schedule 2 to the said Act of 1961 ;

but nothing in this paragraph shall be construed as affecting the validity of a warrant under the said section 15 in relation to a person who has not attained the age of nineteen.

In relation to a person in respect of whom two or more approved school orders would have been in force after the specified day but for sub-paragraph (1) of this paragraph, references to such an order in paragraph (a) of this sub-paragraph are to the later or latest of the orders.

(3) The Secretary of State may from time to time nominate another local authority in the place of a local authority nominated by him in pursuance of the preceding sub-paragraph or this sub-paragraph.

(4) A person who is the subject of a care order by virtue of sub-paragraph (2) of this paragraph and who was unlawfully absent on the specified day from an approved school in which he was then required to be shall, until the local authority to whose care he is committed by the order direct otherwise, be deemed for the purposes

of section 32 of this Act to be duly required by the authority to live after that day in the premises which on that day constituted the school.

(5) A person who on the specified day is the subject of an approved school order or subject to supervision in pursuance of the said Schedule 2 or eligible for assistance under paragraph 7 of that Schedule and is not the subject of a care order from the end of that day by virtue of sub-paragraph (2) of this paragraph shall be deemed for the purposes of section 20 of the Children Act 1948 and section 58 of the Act of 1963 (which authorise local authorities to provide assistance for persons formerly in care) to have been in the care of a local authority under the Children Act 1948 on that day, notwithstanding that he may then have attained the age of eighteen ; and in relation to such a person the reference in the said section 58 to the local authority shall be construed as a reference to any local authority.

(6) If an order under section 88 of the Act of 1933 is in force at the end of the specified day in respect of payments under an affiliation order made for the maintenance of a person who is deemed by virtue of this paragraph to be subject to a care order after that day, the order under that section shall after that day be deemed to have been made, by virtue of the care order, under that section as modified by this Act.

(7) A direction restricting discharge which was given under section 74 of the Mental Health Act 1959 in respect of a person detained by virtue of an approved school order and which is in force at the end of the specified day shall cease to have effect at the end of that day.

(8) References to an approved school order in this paragraph, except in sub-paragraph (2)(*a*), include references to an order of the competent authority under subsection (1) of section 83 of the Act of 1933 and such an order as is mentioned in subsection (3) of that section ; and in relation to those orders this paragraph shall have effect as if for sub-paragraph (2)(*a*) there were substituted the following—

" (*a*) to be the subject of a care order made by a court in England on the date when the order for his detention in a school was made under the relevant law mentioned in section 83 of the Act of 1933 and committing him to the care of a local authority nominated in relation to him by the Secretary of State ; and "

(9) In this paragraph " the specified day " means the day specified for the purposes of section 7(5) of this Act.

8.—(1) An order under the Act of 1933 committing a child or young person to the care of a local authority as a fit person and in force on the date when section 7(6) of this Act comes into force shall be deemed on and after that date to be a care order committing him to the care of that authority.

SCH. 4

(2) Sub-paragraph (6) of the preceding paragraph shall have effect for the purposes of this paragraph as if for references to that paragraph and the specified day there were substituted respectively references to this paragraph and the day preceding the date mentioned in the preceding sub-paragraph.

9. Except as provided by paragraph 1 of this Schedule and this paragraph, nothing in this Act affects—

(a) an order under the Act of 1933 committing a child or young person to the care of a fit person other than a local authority and in force on the date when section 7(6) of this Act comes into force ; or

(b) the operation of any enactment in relation to such an order ;

but where an application for the variation or revocation of the order is considered on or after that date by a juvenile court in pursuance of section 84(6) of the Act of 1933, the court shall have power (to the exclusion of its powers under the said section 84(6)) to refuse the application or to revoke the order and, where it revokes the order, to make a care order in respect of the child or young person in question.

10. Without prejudice to the preceding paragraph, a person who is subject to such an order as is mentioned in sub-paragraph (a) of that paragraph is not a foster-child within the meaning of Part I of the Children Act 1958.

1958 c. 65.

11. Notwithstanding anything in section 20(3) or 21(1) of this Act, an order which is a care order by virtue of paragraph 8 of this Schedule and a care order made by virtue of paragraph 9 of this Schedule shall, unless previously revoked, cease to have effect when the child or young person in question attains the age of eighteen.

12.—(1) Where a supervision order under the Children and Young Persons Acts 1933 to 1963 is in force on the date when this paragraph comes into force or where an order under section 52 of the Act of 1963 (whether made before, on or after that date) falls to be treated by virtue of subsection (3) of that section as a supervision order under the Act of 1933, the order and, in relation to the order, any enactment amended or repealed by this Act shall, subject to the following provisions of this paragraph, have effect as if this Act had not been passed ; and the order may be altered or revoked accordingly.

(2) A juvenile court before which the person to whom such a supervision order relates is brought after the date aforesaid in pursuance of subsection (1) of section 66 of the Act of 1933 shall not have power to make such an order as is mentioned in that subsection in respect of him but shall instead have power to revoke the supervision order and make a care order in respect of him on being satisfied that he is unlikely to receive the care or control he needs unless the court makes a care order ; and section 6(1) of the Act of 1963 shall not apply in a case where the court exercises its power under this sub-paragraph.

(3) Where such a supervision order contains a provision requiring residence in an institution which has become a community home, the

provision shall be construed as requiring residence in the home ; and   SCH. 4
in such a case any reference to an institution of the kind in question
in rules under the Criminal Justice Act 1948 providing for the making   1948 c. 58.
of payments to the body or person by whom the institution is man-
aged shall be construed as a reference to the home.

(4) References to a supervision order in sub-paragraphs (2) and (3)
of this paragraph include references to an order under the said
section 52.

13.—(1) During the period beginning with the coming into force
of section 35 of this Act and ending with the coming into operation
of a regional plan for a particular planning area—

- (a) sections 15 and 16 of the Children Act 1948 shall continue   1948 c. 43.
to apply in relation to each of the relevant authorities ; and

- (b) each of the relevant authorities may continue to exercise the
power conferred by subsection (2) of section 19 of that Act,
as it had effect immediately before the passing of this
Act, to accommodate persons in hostels provided under
that section ; and

- (c) section 77(1) of the Act of 1933 shall continue to apply in
relation to each of the relevant authorities as if for the words
" the duty of " there were substituted the words " lawful
for ".

(2) Where different parts of the area of a local authority are comprised in different planning areas then, in relation to that local
authority, the period specified in sub-paragraph (1) of this paragraph
shall not expire until a regional plan has come into operation for
each of those planning areas.

(3) If on the submission of a regional plan for a planning area to
the Secretary of State part only of the plan is approved by him, any
reference in the preceding provisions of this paragraph to the coming
into operation of a regional plan for that area shall be construed as
a reference to the coming into operation of a further regional plan
containing all necessary supplementary proposals for that area.

14. If immediately before the coming into force of section 49 of
this Act any person has, under section 3(3) of the Children Act 1948,
the care and control of a child (within the meaning of that Act) with
respect to whom a resolution under section 2 of that Act is in
force, then after the coming into force of that section the child shall
again be in the care of the local authority by whom the resolution
was passed but shall be deemed to have been allowed by that
authority, under section 13(2) of that Act (as substituted by the said
section 49), to be under the charge and control of that person, on the
same terms as were applicable under the said section 3(3).

15. It shall be lawful for a person detained in any place in pursuance of section 27 of the Criminal Justice Act 1948 at the time
when paragraph 24 of Schedule 5 to this Act comes into force to be
detained there thereafter, until he is next delivered thence in due
course of law, as if that paragraph had not come into force.

D

Sch. 4
1958 c. 65.
1937 c. 37.
16. Nothing in paragraph 29 of Schedule 5 to this Act affects the operation of section 2(4) of the Children Act 1958 in relation to a supervision order made under the Children and Young Persons (Scotland) Act 1937.

1958 c. 5
(7 & 8 Eliz. 2).
17. Nothing in Schedule 6 to this Act affects the operation of section 15(3) of the Adoption Act 1958 in relation to a fit person order made under the Children and Young Persons (Scotland) Act 1937.

18. Nothing in any provision of Schedule 6 to this Act affects any order which, immediately before the coming into force of that provision, is in force by virtue of any enactment repealed by that provision.

PART II

INTERIM PROVISIONS PENDING COMMENCEMENT OF PROVISIONS OF SOCIAL WORK (SCOTLAND) ACT 1968

1968 c. 49.

19. Where a court in England or Wales by which a child or young person is found guilty of an offence is satisfied that he resides or will reside in Scotland, the court shall have power, without prejudice to its other powers and notwithstanding anything in section 7(2) of this Act, to make a probation order in respect of him in accordance 1948 c. 58. with sections 3 and 9 of the Criminal Justice Act 1948.

20. In section 51(1) of the Act of 1963, for the words " principal Act " there shall be substituted the words " Children and Young Persons Act 1969 in proceedings under section 1 of that Act."

21. In section 51(2) of the Act of 1963, for the words from ".proposes " to " this Act " there shall be substituted ", or a supervision order under the Children and Young Persons Act 1969 has been made in proceedings under section 1 of that Act, proposes to reside or is residing in Scotland " and for the words " specified in the supervision order " there shall be substituted the words " for which the supervision order would have continued in force if it had been allowed to continue in force until it ceased to have effect by the effluxion of time."

22. Where a juvenile court in England or Wales is satisfied that a person who has not attained the age of eighteen and in respect of whom a supervision order made by virtue of section 7(7)(*b*) of this 1949 c. 94. Act or section 7A(4) of the Criminal Justice (Scotland) Act 1949 is in force resides or will reside in Scotland, the court may discharge the order and exercise the like powers to make a probation order in accordance with sections 3 and 9 of the Criminal Justice Act 1948 in respect of him as if in the proceedings it had duly found him guilty of the offence in consequence of which the supervision order was made and section 7(2) of this Act had not been passed ; but a probation order made by virtue of this paragraph shall not continue in force after the date on which the discharged supervision order would have ceased to have effect by the effluxion of time.

23.—(1) Where it appears to the local authority to whose care a person is committed by a care order that his parent or guardian resides or will reside in Scotland and that it is appropriate to transfer him to the care of the managers of an approved school in Scotland, the authority shall make a report on the case to the Secretary of State ; and thereupon the Secretary of State may, if he thinks fit, make an order transferring the person in question to the care of the managers of such a school.

(2) The provisions of the Children and Young Persons (Scotland) Acts 1937 to 1963 shall apply to an order made under this paragraph as if it were an approved school order made by a juvenile court in Scotland on the date on which the care order in question was originally made ; but notwithstanding anything in section 75 of the said Act of 1937 such an order shall cease to have effect on the date when the care order in question would have ceased to have effect by the effluxion of time and the contributions to be made under section 94 of the said Act of 1937 in respect of the person to whom the order under this paragraph relates shall be made by the authority nominated for the purpose in the order under this paragraph, being the education authority within whose area it appears to the Secretary of State at the time that order is made that his parent or guardian resides or will reside.

(3) When a person is received into the care of the managers of an approved school in pursuance of an order under this paragraph, the care order in question shall cease to have effect.

24. If it appears to the Secretary of State that the parent or guardian of a person who has not attained the age of nineteen and is the subject of an approved school order in force under the Children and Young Persons (Scotland) Act 1937, or such other order as is mentioned in subsection (1) or subsection (3) of section 87 of that Act, resides or will reside in the area of a local authority in England or Wales, the Secretary of State may make an order committing that person to the care of that authority ; and an order under this paragraph shall have effect as if it were a care order made on the date on which the approved school or other order was made, but as if sections 20(2) and 21(5) of this Act were omitted.

SCHEDULE 5

MINOR AND CONSEQUENTIAL AMENDMENTS OF ENACTMENTS

The Police (Property) Act 1897

1. The Police (Property) Act 1897 (which makes provision for the disposal of property in the possession of the police) shall apply to property which has come into the possession of the police in connection with an allegation, in proceedings under section 1 of this Act, that the condition set out in subsection (2)(*f*) of that section is satisfied as it applies to property which has come into the possession of the police in the circumstances mentioned in that Act.

The Act of 1933

2. In section 10 of the Act of 1933, after subsection (1) there shall be inserted the following subsection: —

    (1A) Proceedings for an offence under this section shall not be instituted except by a local education authority; and before instituting such proceedings the authority shall consider whether it would be appropriate, instead of or as well as instituting the proceedings, to bring the child or young person in question before a juvenile court under section 1 of the Children and Young Persons Act 1969.

3. In section 34(2) of the Act of 1933, after the words " be taken " there shall be inserted the words " by the person who arrested him ".

4. In section 46 of the Act of 1933, after subsection (1) there shall be inserted the following subsection: —

    (1A) If a notification that the accused desires to plead guilty without appearing before the court is received by the clerk of a court in pursuance of section 1 of the Magistrates' Courts Act 1957 and the court has no reason to believe that the accused is a child or young person, then, if he is a child or young person he shall be deemed to have attained the age of seventeen for the purposes of subsection (1) of this section in its application to the proceedings in question.

5. In section 55(1) of the Act of 1933, for the words " charged with " there shall be substituted the words " found guilty of " and after the word " care " there shall be inserted the words " or control ".

6. In section 56(1) of the Act of 1933, for the word " resides " there shall be substituted the words " habitually resides ".

7. Section 63 of the Act of 1933 shall cease to have effect.

8. In section 86(1) of the Act of 1933 for the words from " an order " to " approved school " there shall be substituted the words " a care order which is not an interim order has been made in respect of a child or young person ".

9.—(1) In subsection (1) of section 87 of the Act of 1933, for the words from " an order has " to " same time, and " there shall be substituted the words " a care order which is not an interim order has been made in respect of a child or young person then, subject to section 62 of the Children and Young Persons Act 1969 ".

(2) For subsection (2) of that section, there shall be substituted the following subsection: —

    (2) A contribution order in respect of a child or young person may be made on the application of the local authority entitled to receive contributions in respect of him.

(3) In subsection (3) of that section for the words from " in the case ", in the first place where they occur, onwards there shall be substituted the words " as long as the child or young person to whom it relates is in the care of the local authority concerned ".

10.—(1) In subsection (1) of section 88 of the Act of 1933 for the words from " ordered " to " approved school " there shall be substituted the words " the subject of a care order (other than an interim order) " ; for the words " that court " there shall be substituted the words " the court which makes the order " ; for the words " the person who is " there shall be substituted the words " the local authority who are ", and for the words " the persons by whom, and in the circumstances in which " there shall be substituted the words " the local authorities by whom ".

(2) In subsection (2)(*c*) of that section, for the words " person who was " there shall be substituted the words " local authority who were ".

(3) In subsection (4) of that section, for paragraphs (*a*) and (*b*) there shall be substituted the words " after the child or young person to whom that order relates has ceased to be the subject of the care order by virtue of which the order under this section was made or, where this section applies by virtue of section 23 of the Children Act 1948, after he has ceased to be in the care of a local authority under section 1 of that Act or, in either case, if he is allowed by the local authority to be under the charge and control of a parent, guardian, relative or friend, although remaining in the care of the local authority ".

11. In section 106(2)(*a*) of the Act of 1933, for the words from " fifty-seven " to " Schedule to " there shall be substituted the words " eighty-seven and eighty-eight of ".

12.—(1) In section 107(1) of the Act of 1933, after the words " that is to say " there shall be inserted the following words : —

> " care order " and " interim order " have the same meanings as in the Children and Young Persons Act 1969.

(2) In the said section 107(1), in the definition of " place of safety ", for the words " any home provided by a local authority under Part II of the Children Act 1948 any remand home or " there shall be substituted the words " a community home provided by a local authority or a controlled community home, any ".

(3) Section 107(2) of the Act of 1933 shall cease to have effect.

The Education Act 1944

13. For subsections (2) to (5) of section 40 of the Education Act 1944 there shall be substituted the following subsections : —

> (2) Proceedings for such offences as aforesaid shall not be instituted except by a local education authority ; and before instituting such proceedings the authority shall

E

consider whether it would be appropriate, instead of or as well as instituting the proceedings, to bring the child in question before a juvenile court under section 1 of the Children and Young Persons Act 1969.

(3) The court by which a person is convicted of an offence against section 37 of this Act or before which a person is charged with an offence against section 39 of this Act may if it thinks fit direct the authority who instituted the proceedings to bring the child to whom the proceedings relate before a juvenile court under the said section 1 ; and it shall be the duty of the authority to comply with the direction.

(4) Where a child in respect of whom a school attendance order is in force is brought before a juvenile court by a local education authority under the said section 1 and the court finds that the condition set out in subsection (2)(*e*) of that section is not satisfied with respect to him, the court may direct that the order shall cease to be in force.

The Children Act 1948

14. In section 4(3) of the Children Act 1948, the proviso shall cease to have effect.

15. In section 20(1) of the said Act of 1948, for the words " any such person as is mentioned in subsection (1) of the last foregoing section " there shall be substituted the words " any person over compulsory school age but under the age of twenty one who is, or has at any time after ceasing to be of compulsory school age been, in the care of a local authority ".

16. In section 23(1) of the said Act of 1948 for the words from " committed " in the second place where it occurs to the end of the subsection there shall be substituted the words " in the care of a local authority by virtue of such an order as is mentioned in sub-section (1) of the said section 86 ".

17.—(1) In section 26(1) of the said Act of 1948 for paragraph (*b*) there shall be substituted the following paragraph: —

(*b*) an illegitimate child is in the care of a local authority by virtue of such an order as is mentioned in section 86(1) of the Children and Young Persons Act 1933, or.

(2) In subsections (3) and (4)(*b*) of the said section 26, for the words " person who is " there shall be substituted the words " local authority who are ", and in subsection (4) of that section for the words " (*b*) or (*c*) " there shall be substituted the words " or (*b*) ".

18. In section 39(1) of the said Act of 1948 after paragraph (*h*) there shall be inserted the following paragraph: —

(*i*) the Children and Young Persons Act 1969.

Scн. 5
1958 c. 5
(7 & 8 Eliz. 2).
1968 c.53.

19. In section 43(1) of the said Act of 1948 for the words from " Parts IV and V " onwards there shall be substituted the words " the Children and Young Persons Acts 1933 to 1969, the Adoption Act 1958 and the Adoption Act 1968 ".

20.—(1) In subsection (1) of section 51 of the said Act of 1948, for the words from " homes " to " this Act " there shall be substituted the words " community homes provided by them or in controlled community homes " and at the end of that subsection there shall be added the words " or sections 2(5), 16(3) or 28 of the Children and Young Persons Act 1969 and of children detained by them in pursuance of arrangements under section 29(3) of that Act ".

(2) In subsection (3) of the said section 51, for the words from " home " to ·" this Act " there shall be substituted the words " community home provided by a local authority or a controlled community home ".

21.—(1) In subsection (3) of section 54 of the said Act of 1948, after the word " area " in the first place where it occurs there shall be inserted the words " other than community homes " and after the word " any " in the last place where it occurs, there shall be inserted the word " such ".

(2) In subsection (4) of that section, for the words from " as a fit person " to the end of the subsection there shall be substituted the words " by a care order within the meaning of the Children and Young Persons Act 1969 or by a warrant under section 23(1) of that Act."

(3) In subsection (5) of that section, for the words from " ninety-four " to " 1933 " there shall be substituted the words " section 58 of the Children and Young Persons Act 1969 ".

22. In section 59(1) of the said Act of 1948, at the end of the definition of " child " there shall be added the words " and any person who has attained that age and is the subject of a care order within the meaning of the Children and Young Persons Act 1969 ".

The Criminal Justice Act 1948

1948 c. 58.

23. In section 19(1) of the Criminal Justice Act 1948, after the words " who is " there shall be inserted the words " not less than seventeen but ".

24. For section 27 of the said Act of 1948 there shall be substituted the following section : —

Remand of persons aged 17 to 20.

27.—(1) Where a court remands a person charged with or convicted of an offence or commits him for trial or sentence and he is not less than seventeen but under twenty-one years old and is not released on bail, then, if the court has been notified by the Secretary of State that a remand centre is available for the reception from

SCH. 5

the court of persons of his class or description, it shall commit him to a remand centre and, if it has not been so notified, it shall commit him to a prison.

(2) Where a person is committed to a remand centre in pursuance of this section, the centre shall be specified in the warrant and he shall be detained there for the period for which he is remanded or until he is delivered thence in due course of law.

1952 c. 55.

(3) In this section " court " includes a justice ; and nothing in this section affects the provisions of section 105(5) of the Magistrates' Courts Act 1952 (which provides for remands to the custody of a constable).

1949 c. 94.

The Criminal Justice (Scotland) Act 1949

25. In section 7 of the Criminal Justice (Scotland) Act 1949, after the words " that the offender " in subsection (1) and " that the probationer " in subsection (2) there shall be inserted the words " has attained the age of seventeen and ".

26. After section 7 of the said Act of 1949 there shall be inserted the following section : —

Further provisions as to probation orders relating to persons residing or formerly residing in England.

7A.—(1) Where the court by which a probation order is made under section 2 of this Act or subsection (6) of this section is satisfied that the person to whom the order relates is under the age of seventeen and resides or will reside in England, subsection (2) of the said section 2 shall not apply to the order but the order shall name the petty sessions area in which that person resides or will reside and the court shall send notification of the order to the clerk to the justices for that area.

(2) Where a probation order has been made under section 2 of this Act or subsection (6) of this section and the court which made the order or the appropriate court is satisfied that the person to whom the order relates is under the age of seventeen and proposes to reside or is residing in England, the power of that court to amend the order under Schedule 2 to this Act shall include power, without summoning him and without his consent, to insert in the order the name of the petty sessions area aforesaid ; and where the court exercises the power conferred on it by virtue of this subsection it shall send notification of the order to the clerk aforesaid.

(3) A court which sends a notification to a clerk in pursuance of the foregoing provisions of this section shall send to him with it three copies of the probation order in question and such other documents and information relating to the case as it considers likely to be of assistance to the juvenile court mentioned in the following subsection.

(4) It shall be the duty of the clerk to whom a notification is sent in pursuance of the foregoing provisions of this section to refer the notification to a juvenile court acting for the petty sessions area named in the order, and on such a reference the court—

    (*a*) may make a supervision order under the Children and Young Persons Act 1969 in respect of a person to whom the notification relates ; and

    (*b*) if it does not make such an order, shall dismiss the case.

(5) A supervision order made by virtue of the foregoing subsection shall not include a requirement authorised by section 12 of the said Act of 1969 unless the supervised person is before the court when the supervision order is made, and in relation to a supervision order made by virtue of that subsection—

    (*a*) section 15 of that Act shall have effect as if in subsection (4) paragraph (*b*) and the words following it were omitted ; and

    (*b*) section 17(*a*) of that Act shall have effect as if the second reference to the supervision order were a reference to the probation order in consequence of which the supervision order is made ;

and when a juvenile court disposes of a case referred to it in pursuance of the foregoing subsection, the probation order in consequence of which the reference was made shall cease to have effect.

(6) The court which, in pursuance of subsection (1) of section 73 of the Social Work (Scotland) Act 1968, considers a case referred to it in consequence of a notification under paragraph (i) of that subsection (which relates to a case in which a person subject to a supervision order made by virtue of this section moves to Scotland)— 1968 c. 49.

    (*a*) may, if it is of opinion that the person to whom the notification relates should continue to be under supervision, make a probation order in respect of him for a period specified in the order ; and

    (*b*) if it does not make such an order, shall dismiss the case ;

and when the court disposes of a case in pursuance of this subsection the supervision order aforesaid shall cease to have effect.

(7) Notwithstanding any provision to the contrary in section 2 of this Act, a probation order made by virtue of the foregoing subsection which includes only requirements having the like effect as any requirement or provision of the supervision order to which the notification

relates may be made without summoning the person to
whom the notification relates and without his consent,
and shall specify a period of supervision which shall
expire not later than the date on which that supervision
order would have ceased to have effect by the effluxion
of time ; and, except as aforesaid, Part I of this Act shall
apply to that probation order.

(8) In this section " petty sessions area " has the same
meaning as in the said Act of 1969.

The Sexual Offences Act 1956

27. In section 37(7) of the Sexual Offences Act 1956, for the words
" section twenty or twenty-one of the Magistrates' Courts Act 1952
(which relate " in paragraph (a) there shall be substituted the words
" section 6 of the Children and Young Persons Act 1969 (which
relates " and for the words " that Act " in paragraph (b) there shall
be substituted the words " the Magistrates' Courts Act 1952 ".

The Affiliation Proceedings Act 1957

28.—(1) In section 5(2)(a) of the Affiliation Proceedings Act 1957,
for the words from " fit person " to " school " there shall be substituted the words " local authority ".

(2) In section 7(4) of that Act, for paragraph (a) there shall be
substituted the following paragraph : —
    (a) subject to the next following subsection, so as to require
      payments thereunder to be made in respect of any period
      when the child is in the care of a local authority under
      section 1 of the Children Act 1948 or by virtue of a care
      order (other than an interim order) within the meaning
      of the Children and Young Persons Act 1969 ;

(3) In section 7(6) of that Act, for the words from " a person "
onwards there shall be subsituted the words " by virtue of such a
care order as aforesaid ".

The Children Act 1958

29. In section 2(4) of the Children Act 1958, for the words
" supervision order or " there shall be substituted the words " supervision order within the meaning of the Children and Young Persons
Act 1969 or a ".

30. In section 9 of the said Act of 1958, after the words " foster
child " there shall be inserted the words " for reward ".

31. In section 12(1) of the said Act of 1958, for the words " one
month " there shall be substituted the words " two weeks ".

32. In section 17 of the said Act of 1958, after the words " that is
to say " there shall be inserted the words " " approved school " has
the same meaning as in the Children and Young Persons (Scotland)

Act 1937 ; " and, in the definition of " place of safety ", for the word
" home " in the first place where it occurs there shall be substituted
the words " community home " and for the words " under Part II
of the Children Act 1948, remand " there shall be substituted the
words " a controlled community ".

The Adoption Act 1958

33.—(1) In section 4(3) of the Adoption Act 1958, for paragraph
(a) there shall be substituted the following paragraph : —

> (a) section 24 of the Children and Young Persons Act 1969
> (which relates to the powers and duties of local authorities
> with respect to persons committed to their care in pursuance
> of that Act).

34. In section 15(3) of the said Act of 1958, for the words " the
last mentioned order " there shall be substituted the words " or to
the care of a local authority by a care order (other than an interim
order) in force under the Children and Young Persons Act 1969,
the fit person order or care order as the case may be ".

35. In section 37(2) of the said Act of 1958, for the words " (4) or
(5) " there shall be substituted the words " or (4) ".

36. In section 57(1) of the said Act of 1958, in the definition of
" place of safety ", for the word " home " in the first place where
it occurs there shall be substituted the words " community home "
and for the words " under Part II of the Children Act 1948, remand "
there shall be substituted the words " a controlled community ".

The Mental Health Act 1959

37.—(1) In subsection (1) of section 9 of the Mental Health Act
1959 for the words from " or other accommodation " to " section
fifteen of that Act " there shall be substituted the words " as provided
under section 38 of the Children and Young Persons Act 1969 " and
for the words " that Act " there shall be substituted the words " the
Children Act 1948 ".

(2) In subsection (2) of the said section 9, for the words " or other
accommodation provided under the said section fifteen " there shall
be substituted the words " provided under the said section 38 ".

38. In section 10(1)(a) of the said Act of 1959 for sub-paragraph
(i) there shall be substituted the following sub-paragraph : —

> (i) section 24 of the Children and Young Persons Act 1969
> (which relates to the powers and duties of local authorities
> with respect to persons committed to their care in pursuance
> of that Act).

39. In section 50 of the said Act of 1959, for paragraph (a) there
shall be substituted the following paragraph : —

> (a) section 24 of the Children and Young Persons Act 1969
> (which relates to the powers and duties of local authorities

SCH. 5

with respect to persons committed to their care in pursuance of that Act).

40. In section 60(6) of the said Act of 1959, after the word " offence " there shall be inserted the words " or make any such order as is mentioned in paragraphs (*b*) or (*c*) of section 7(7) of the Children and Young Persons Act 1969 in respect of the offender ".

41. In section 62(4) of the said Act of 1959 for the words " section 62 of the Children and Young Persons Act 1933 " there shall be substituted the words " section 1 of the Children and Young Persons Act 1969 ".

1960 c. 61.

The Mental Health (Scotland) Act 1960

42. In section 10(1)(*a*) of the Mental Health (Scotland) Act 1960, for sub-paragraph (ii) there shall be substituted the following sub-paragraph: —

(ii)   section 24 of the Children and Young Persons Act 1969 (which relates to the powers and duties of local authorities in England and Wales with respect to persons committed to their care).

43. In section 46 of the said Act of 1960, for paragraph (*b*) there shall be substituted the following paragraph: —

(*b*)   section 24 of the Children and Young Persons Act 1969 (which relates to the powers and duties of local authorities in England and Wales with respect to persons committed to their care).

1961 c. 39.

The Criminal Justice Act 1961

44. For section 5(1) of the Criminal Justice Act 1961 there shall be substituted the following: —

Defaulters already detained in detention centre.

5.—(1) Where a court has power to commit a person to prison for any term for a default and that person has attained the age of seventeen and is detained in a detention centre under a previous sentence or warrant, the court may, subject to the provisions of this section, commit him to a detention centre for a term not exceeding the term aforesaid or six months, whichever is the shorter.

and subsection (3) of section 6 of that Act shall be subsection (6) of section 5 of that Act.

45. In section 9 of the said Act of 1961, for the words from the beginning to " that Act ", where they first occur, there shall be substituted the words " Where an order for conditional discharge under section seven of the Criminal Justice Act 1948 ".

1948 c. 58.

46. In section 29(3)(*a*) of the said Act of 1961, for the words " that Act " there shall be substituted the words " the Children and Young Persons Act 1933 ".

The Act of 1963

47. In section 3(1) of the Act of 1963, for the words " section 62 of the principal Act " there shall be substituted the words " section 1 of the Children and Young Persons Act 1969 ".

48. In section 23 of the Act of 1963, in subsection (1)(*b*), for the words " that Act " there shall be substituted the words " the principal Act " and, in subsection (5), for the words from " for his detention " onwards there shall be substituted the words " within the meaning of the Children and Young Persons Act 1969 ".

49. In section 29(1) of the Act of 1963, for the words " before a juvenile court under section 62 or section 65 of the principal Act " there shall be substituted the words " under section 1 of the Children and Young Persons Act 1969 or for an offence " ; and section 29(2) of the Act of 1963 shall cease to have effect.

50.—(1) In subsection (1) of section 30 of the Act of 1963, for the words " the person who " there shall be substituted the words " the local authority who ".

(2) In subsection (3) of that section, for the words " subsections (3) and (4) " there shall be substituted " subsection (3) " and at the end of that subsection there shall be added the words " section 62 of the Children and Young Persons Act 1969 ".

(3) In subsection (4) of that section for the words from " a magistrates' court ", in the first place where they occur, to the end of the subsection there shall be substituted the words " a magistrates' court acting for the area or part of the area of the local authority which is the applicant."

(4) In subsection (5) of that section for the words " 14(1) of this Act keep the person " there shall be substituted the words " 24(8) of the Children and Young Persons Act 1969 keep the local authority ".

51. In section 45(1) of the Act of 1963, after the words " the Children Act 1958 " there shall be inserted the words " the Children and Young Persons Act 1969 ".

52. In section 49(1) of the Act of 1963, for the words " section 3(3) ", there shall be substituted the words " section 13(2) " and for the words " over the care " in both places there shall be substituted the word " charge ".

53. For subsection (3) of section 57 of the Act of 1963 there shall be substituted the following subsection : —

(3) The said sections 39 and 49 shall extend to Scotland and the said sections 46 and 54 shall extend to England and Wales, but—

(*a*) references to a court in the said sections 39 and 49 shall not include a court in Scotland ; and (*b*) references to a court in the said sections 46 and 54 shall not include a court in England or Wales.

The Family Allowances Act 1965

54.—(1) In subsection (1)(*b*) of section 11 of the Family Allowances Act 1965, for the words " said Act of " there shall be substituted the words " Children and Young Persons Act ".

(2) In subsection (2) of that section for the words " said Act of 1933 " there shall be substituted the words " Children and Young Persons Act 1969 (other than an interim order) " and for the words from " 5(1) " to " 1956 " there shall be substituted the words " 13(2) of the Children Act 1948 ".

(3) In subsection (3) of that section, for the words " 3 or 4 " there shall be substituted the words " 4 or 13(2) ".

The Criminal Justice Act 1967

55. In sections 2 and 9 of the Criminal Justice Act 1967, after subsection (3) of each section there shall be inserted the following subsection : —

(3A) In the case of a statement which indicates in pursuance of subsection (3)(*a*) of this section that the person making it has not attained the age of fourteen, subsection (2)(*b*) of this section shall have effect as if for the words from " made " onwards there were substituted the words " understands the importance of telling the truth in it."

56. In section 3(3) of the Criminal Justice Act 1967, for the words " 19 or 20 of the Magistrates' Courts Act 1952 " there shall be substituted the words " or 19 of the Magistrates' Courts Act 1952 or section 6 of the Children and Young Persons Act 1969 ".

The Social Work (Scotland) Act 1968

57. After section 44(1) of the Social Work (Scotland) Act 1968, there shall be inserted the following subsection : —

(1A) A supervision requirement imposing a condition as to the place where a child is to reside in England or Wales shall be a like authority as in Scotland for the person in charge of the place to restrict the child's liberty to such an extent as that person may consider appropriate having regard to the terms of the supervision requirement.

58.—(1) In section 72 of the said Act of 1968, after subsection (1) there shall be inserted the following subsection : —

(1A) The juvenile court in England or Wales to which notification of a supervision requirement is sent under this section may make a supervision order in respect of the person to whom the notification relates but, notwithstanding anything in section 76(1) of this Act, shall not include in the order a requirement authorised by section 12 of the Children and Young Persons

Act 1969 unless that person is before the court when the supervision order is made ; and in relation to a supervision order
made by virtue of this subsection—

    (*a*) section 15 of that Act shall have effect as if subsection
        (2) were omitted ; and

    (*b*) section 17 of that Act shall have effect as if in paragraph
        (*a*) the references to three years and the date on which
        the order was originally made were respectively refer-
        ences to one year and the date on which the said
        notification was sent and as if in paragraph (*b*) the
        words from " the order was " to " and " were omitted.

(2) In subsection (2) of that section, after the word " court " there
shall be inserted the words " in Northern Ireland ".

(3) In subsection (4) of that section for the words from " includes "
to " 1963 " there shall be substituted the words ", in relation to
England and Wales, has the same meaning as in the said Act of
1969 ".

59.—(1) In section 73 of the said Act of 1968, in subsection (1),
after the word " reporter ", in the second place where it occurs, there
shall be inserted the following words : —

    (i) in the case of a supervision order made by virtue of
section 7A(4) of the Criminal Justice (Scotland) Act 1949, to 1949 c. 94.
notify the appropriate court and to transmit to that court all
documents and certified copies of documents relating to the
case which the reporter has received by virtue of section 76 of
this Act ;

    (ii) in any other case.
and at the end of that subsection there shall be inserted the following
paragraph : —

    In this subsection " the appropriate court " means the sheriff
having jurisdiction in the area in which the child proposes to
reside or is residing or, where the original probation order was
imposed by the High Court of Justiciary, that Court.

(2) After subsection (1) of that section there shall be inserted the
following subsection : —

    (1A) Where a court in England or Wales is satisfied that a
child in respect of whom the court proposes to make a supervision order is residing or proposes to reside in Scotland, the
court may make the order notwithstanding anything in subsection
(1) of section 18 of the Children and Young Persons Act 1969
(which relates to residence of the supervised person in England
or Wales) ; and where the court makes a supervision order by
virtue of this subsection—

    (*a*) the areas to be named in the order in pursuance of sub-
        section (2)(*a*) of the said section 18 shall be those in
        which the court is sitting ;

    (*b*) the order may require the supervised person to
        comply with directions of the supervisor with respect to

his departure to Scotland, and any such requirement shall, for the purposes of sections 15 and 16 of that Act (which relate to the variation and discharge of supervision orders), be deemed to be included in the order in pursuance of section 12(2) of that Act ; and

(c) the court shall send notification of the order as mentioned in paragraph (b) of the foregoing subsection and the provisions of that subsection relating to the duty of the reporter shall apply accordingly.

(3) In subsection (2) of that section for the word " subsection " there shall be substituted the words " provisions of this section."

60. In section 74 of the said Act of 1968, after subsection (5) there shall be inserted the following subsection : —

(6) An order under this section committing a child to the care of a local authority shall have effect as if it were a care order under the Children and Young Persons Act 1969, but as if sections 20(2) and 21(5) of that Act and in section 20(3) of that Act paragraph (a) and the words ' in any other case ' in paragraph (b) were omitted.

61.—(1) In section 75 of the said Act of 1968, in subsection (1) after the word " order " there shall be inserted the words " or an order under section 74(3) of this Act relating to a training school ".

(2) In subsection (2) of that section, for the words from " under ", where it first occurs, to " 1944 " there shall be substituted the words " by a care order (other than an interim order) within the meaning of the Children and Young Persons Act 1969 or an order under section 74(3) of this Act " and after the word " 1947 " there shall be inserted the words " or the said section 74(3) ".

(3) In subsection (3) of that section, after the words " training school order " there shall be inserted the words " or order under the said section 74(3) relating to a training school ".

(4) In subsection (4) of that section after the word " order " there shall be inserted the words " under the said section 74(3) or ".

62. In section 76(4) of the said Act of 1968, after the word " order " there shall be inserted the words " or order under section 74(3) of this Act relating to a training school ".

63. In section 90(1) of the said Act of 1968, the words " or to prescribe any matter," shall be omitted.

64. In section 94(1) of the said Act of 1968—

(1) after the definition of " place of safety " there shall be inserted the words—

" prescribed " means—

(a) in section 3, prescribed by regulations,

(b) in section 44, prescribed by rules, and

(c) in sections 62(2), 66(1) and (2), 94, paragraphs 2(2) and (3), 4(3) and (4) of Schedule 7, prescribed by order,

(2) in the definition of "supervision order" after the word "1963" there shall be inserted the words "and includes a supervision order within the meaning of the Children and Young Persons Act 1969".

65. In section 97(1) of the said Act of 1968—

(1) after the words "that is to say—" there shall be inserted the words "section 44(1) (except head (*b*)) and (1A)",

(2) after the words "Part V" there shall be inserted the words "section 98(3)" and "Schedule 2, paragraphs 7 and 13".

66. In section 98 of the said Act of 1968, after subsection (2) there shall be inserted the following subsection:—

(3) An order under this section may make such transitional provisions as appear to the Secretary of State to be necessary or expedient in connection with the provisions thereby brought into force, including such adaptations of those provisions or of any provision of this Act then in force as appear to the Secretary of State necessary or expedient for the purposes or in consequence of the operation of any provision of this Act before the coming into force of any other provision of this Act or of the Children and Young Persons Act 1969.

67. In Schedule 2 to the said Act of 1968, in paragraph 10, to section 50 of the Children and Young Persons (Scotland) Act 1937 1937 c. 37. as substituted by that paragraph, there shall be added the following subsection:—

(2) The provisions of the foregoing subsection so far as they relate to section 54 of this Act shall extend to England and Wales.

68. In Schedule 2 to the said Act of 1968, in paragraph 19, after the word "'children'" there shall be inserted the words ", for the word 'offenders' there shall be substituted the word 'children', and for the word 'offender' in the three places where that word occurs there shall be substituted the word 'child'".

69. In Schedule 7 to the said Act of 1968, in paragraph 1(1)(*a*), for the words "section 63" there shall be substituted the words "section 62".

70. In Schedule 8 to the said Act of 1968, in paragraph 7—

(*a*) for sub-paragraph (1) of that paragraph there shall be substituted the following sub-paragraph:—

(1) In section 87, for subsection (1), there shall be substituted the following subsection—

(1) Any person detained in a training school under the law in force in Northern Ireland may, with the consent of the Secretary of State, be transferred by order of the competent authority in Northern Ireland to such place in Scotland as the Secretary of State may direct for the purposes of undergoing residential training, and shall be

subject to the provisions of this Act and of the Criminal Justice (Scotland) Act 1963 as if the order sending him to the school in Northern Ireland were an order for committal for residential training made under section 58A of this Act made upon the same date, and as if the order were an authority for his detention for a period not exceeding the period for which he might be detained under the training school order made in respect of him.;

(*b*) in sub-paragraph (2) of that paragraph at the end there shall be inserted the words " ; and in section 87(2) and (4) the words " England or ", wherever they occur, shall be omitted " ;

(*c*) in sub-paragraph (3) of that paragraph the words " to such " shall be omitted ;

(*d*) after sub-paragraph (3) of that paragraph there shall be inserted the following sub-paragraphs—

(4) In section 87(5) the words " in relation to England, the Secretary of State, and," shall be omitted.

(5) In section 87 subsection (6) shall be omitted.

71. In Schedule 8 to the said Act of 1968, in paragraph 9(2), for the word " for " there shall be substituted the word " of ".

72. In Schedule 8 to the said Act of 1968, in paragraph 10, at the end there shall be inserted the following words—

" after the definition of " Street " there shall be inserted the following definition—

' Training school order ' has the same meaning as in the Social Work (Scotland) Act 1968 "

73. In Schedule 8 to the said Act of 1968, in paragraph 17(1), for the words " in Scotland " there shall be substituted the words ", within the meaning of the Social Work (Scotland) Act 1968 ".

74. In Schedule 8 to the said Act of 1968, in paragraph 38, for the words " In section 15(4) " there shall be substituted the words—
" (1) In section 15(3), for the words " the last mentioned order " there shall be substituted the words " or to the care of a local authority by a care order (other than an interim order) in force under the Children and Young Persons Act 1969, the fit person order or care order as the case may be ".
(2) In subsection (4) ".

75. In Schedule 8 to the said Act of 1968, in sub-paragraph (1) of paragraph 51, for the words from " include " where it secondly occurs to the end of the sub-paragraph there shall be substituted the words " include ' ; and paragraph (*e*) shall be omitted."

76. In Schedule 8 to the said Act of 1968, in paragraph 54, for the word " and " where that word first occurs there shall be substituted the word " or " and after the words " " by virtue of " " there shall be inserted the words " where those words secondly occur ".

77. In Schedule 8 to the said Act of 1968, after paragraph 59, there shall be inserted the following paragraph:— Sch. 5

Criminal Justice Act 1961 1961 c. 39.

59A. In section 32(2), after paragraph (g), there shall be inserted the following paragraph—

> (h) section 58A of the Children and Young Persons 1937 c. 37. (Scotland) Act 1937.

78. In Schedule 8 to the said Act of 1968, for paragraph 74(1), there shall be substituted the following sub-paragraph—

74.—(1) For section 11(1)(a) there shall be substituted the following paragraph—

> (a) during which his or her residence in a residential establishment is required by a supervision requirement made under section 44 of the Social Work (Scotland) Act 1968, and the child is not absent from 1968 c. 49. the residential establishment under supervision ;

in paragraph (b), for the words " the said Act of 1937 " there shall be substituted the words " the Children and Young Persons (Scotland) Act 1937 ", after paragraph (b) there shall be inserted the following paragraph :—

> (bb) during which the child is liable to undergo residential training under committal by virtue of section 58A of the said Act of 1937, and is not released under that section ;

and for paragraph (c) there shall be substituted the following paragraph :—

> (c) during which the child is accommodated by virtue of rules made by the Secretary of State under section 45 of the Social Work (Scotland) Act 1968 ".

79. In Part I of Schedule 9 to the said Act of 1968, in the entry relating to the Children and Young Persons (Scotland) Act 1937, in the third column, after the words " Sections 68 to 86 " there shall be inserted the following words : —

> " In section 87(2) and (4) the words " England or " wherever they occur, in subsection (5) the words " in relation to England, the Secretary of State, and " and subsection (6)."

80. In Part I of Schedule 9 to the said Act of 1968, in the entry relating to the Children Act 1958, in the third column, for the words " Section 2(6) and (7) " there shall be substituted the words—

> In section 2, in subsection (4) the words from " or by virtue of " to " of an approved school ", and subsections (6) and (7).

81. In Part I of Schedule 9 to the said Act of 1968, in the entry relating to section 15(3) of the Adoption Act 1958, in the third 1958 c. 5 column, for the words " ' or the Children ' to ' 1937 ' " there shall (7 & 8 Eliz. 2). be substituted the following words " ' fit person by ' to ' care of a ' and the words ' fit person order or ' and ' as the case may be ' ".

SCH. 5   82. In Part II of Schedule 9 to the said Act of 1968, in the entry relating to the Children Act 1958, in the third column, the entry relating to section 17 shall be omitted.

83. In Part II of Schedule 9 to the said Act of 1968, in the entry relating to the Family Allowances Act 1965, in the third column, for the words from " 11," to " (2)," there shall be substituted the word " 11(2),".

Section 72(4).

SCHEDULE 6

REPEALS

Chapter	Short title	Extent of repeal
1894 c. 60.	The Merchant Shipping Act 1894.	In section 183(3), the proviso.
1918 c. 57.	The War Pensions (Administrative Provisions) Act 1918.	Section 9(4).
1920 c. 23.	The War Pensions Act 1920.	Section 9.
1933 c. 12.	The Children and Young Persons Act 1933.	In section 10(2) the words from " and may " onwards. Sections 26(6), 29(3) and 32. In section 34(2) the words " or taken to a place of safety ". Section 35. In section 44, in subsection (1) the words from " being " to " as ", and subsection (2). In section 48(2) the words " a probationer or " and " any failure to comply with the requirements of the probation order or " and the words from " or to amend " onwards. Section 54. In section 55 the words " child or " wherever they occur, in subsection (1) the words " in any case and shall if the offender is a child," subsection (2), and in subsection (4) the words " or on forfeiture of any such security as aforesaid ". In section 56(1) the words " child or ". Sections 57 and 58. In section 59(1) the words " children and " and " child or ". Sections 62 to 85.

Children and Young Persons Act 1969   Cн. **54**   113

Chapter	Short title	Extent of repeal
1933 c. 12— *cont.*	The Children and Young Persons Act 1933—*cont.*	In section 86, subsection (2), in subsection (3) the words " or ordered to be sent to an approved school " and the words from " and ", in the first place where it occurs, to the end of the subsection, and subsection (4). Sections 89(1), 90, 91 and 94. In section 102, paragraphs (*a*) and (*b*) of subsection (1), and in subsection (2) the words from " the rights " to " Act or ". Sections 103 and 104. In section 106, subsections (3) to (5). In section 107(1) the definitions of " approved school ", " approved school order ", " managers " and " special reception centre ". Section 107(2). Section 108(2) and (3). Schedule 4.
1937 c. 37.	The Children and Young Persons (Scotland) Act 1937.	Sections 82, 86, 87 and 89. In Schedule 2, paragraph 13.
1938 c. 40.	The Children and Young Persons Act 1938.	The whole Act.
1944 c. 31.	The Education Act 1944.	Section 40A.
1948 c. 33.	The Superannuation (Mis- cellaneous Provisions) Act 1948.	Section 14.
1948 c. 40.	The Education (Miscel- laneous Provisions) Act 1948.	In Schedule 1, the entries relating to section 40 of the Education Act 1944.
1948 c. 43.	The Children Act 1948.	Section 3(3) to (5). In section 4(3), the proviso. Sections 5, 6(3) and (4), 7, 15 and 16. In section 23, in subsection (1), the words from " (which " to " aliment) " and subsection (3). Section 25. In section 26(1), paragraph (*c*), and in paragraph (ii) the words " or (*c*) " and the words from " or ", in the second place where it occurs, on- wards. Section 39(1)(*e*). In section 49(1), the words from " other than " onwards. Section 51(2). Section 54(1) and (2).

Chapter	Short title	Extent of repeal
1948 c. 43—*cont.*	The Children Act 1948—*cont.*	In section 59, in subsection (1) the definition of " approved school order ", and subsection (2). In Schedule 3, the entries relating to sections 70, 82, 84, 90 and 107 of the Act of 1933.
1948 c. 58.	The Criminal Justice Act 1948.	In section 3(5), the words from " if the " to " age ". In section 11(1) the words from the beginning to " behaviour " in the first place where it occurs. In sections 46(1) and 47(1) the words " or a supervision order". Sections 48(4), 49, 71, 72 and 75. In section 77, in subsection (1) the words " or in remand homes or approved schools ", in subsection (4)(c) the words " in remand homes or " and " or in approved schools ", and subsection (6). In section 80(1), the definitions of " approved school " " remand home " and " supervision order " and in the definition of " sentence " the words from " an ", in the second place where it occurs, to " school ". In Schedule 9, the entries relating to sections 54, 58, 70, 77, 78, 82 and 90 of the Act of 1933, in the entry relating to section 48(2) of the Act of 1933 the words " a probationer or " and " any failure to comply with the requirements of the probation order or " and the words from " or to amend " to the end of the entry, and the entry relating to the Children and Young Persons Act 1938.
1949 c. 101.	The Justices of the Peace Act 1949.	Section 14.
1950 c. 37.	The Maintenance Orders Act 1950.	In Schedule 1, in the entry relating to section 86 of the Act of 1933, the words from " or as " onwards.
1952 c. 50.	The Children and Young Persons (Amendment) Act 1952.	Sections 2 to 5. In the Schedule, paragraphs 2, 3, 5 ,8, 9 and 11 to 16.

Chapter	Short title	Extent of repeal
1952 c. 52.	The Prison Act 1952.	In section 49(2) the words " remand home or", where they first occur, and the words " remand home " wherever else they occur. In section 50, the words from " and subsection " onwards. In section 53(1) the definition of " remand home ".
1952 c. 55.	The Magistrates' Courts Act 1952.	Sections 20, 21 and 26(2). Section 32. In section 38(1), the words from " The provisions of this " onwards.
1953 c. 33.	The Education (Miscellaneous Provisions) Act 1953.	Section 11.
1956 c. 24.	The Children and Young Persons Act 1956.	The whole Act.
1956 c. 50.	The Family Allowances and National Insurance Act 1956.	Section 5.
1957 c. 55.	The Affiliation Proceedings Act 1957.	In section 5(2)(*d*) the words from " or " onwards. In section 7(5), the words " Sub-paragraph (ii) of ".
1958 c. 55.	The Local Government Act 1958.	In Schedule 8, in paragraph 2, sub-paragraph (3), in sub-paragraph (4) the words " paragraph (*b*) of ", and sub-paragraph (5).
1958 c. 65.	The Children Act 1958.	In section 2, in subsection (1) the words from " for reward " to " one month ", in subsection (2) the words from " by " in the first place where it occurs to " or " where that word first subsequently occurs, in subsection (4) the words " the Children and Young Persons Act 1933 or of ", and subsections (6) and (7). In section 3, in subsection (4), the words from " or is removed " to " maintaining him " and the words from " or removal " onwards, in subsection (5) the words " need not give a notice under subsection (4) of this section but ", and subsection (6). In section 17, in the definition of " fit person order " the words " the Children and Young Persons Act 1933 or ". In Schedule 2 the entry relating to section 54 of the Children Act 1948.

Chapter	Short title	Extent of repeal
1958 c. 5 (7 & 8 Eliz. 2).	The Adoption Act 1958	In section 15(3) the words from " fit person by " to " care of a " and the words " fit person order or " and " as the case may be ". In section 37, in subsection (1) the words " but is not a foster child within the meaning of Part I of the Children Act 1958 ", in subsection (2) the words from " by reason " to "subsection nor", and in subsection (3) the words " in an approved school or ".
1959 c. 72.	The Mental Health Act 1959.	In section 60(6) the words from " including " onwards. Section 61. Section 70(2). In section 72(6)(*a*) the words from " or made " to " Act 1933 " and from " or an order " onwards. In section 75(1), the words "(other than a person detained in a remand home) " and in paragraph (*b*) the words from " or as " to " have been remitted ", and in section 75(2) the words from " including " to " 1963 ". Section 79. In section 80(1), the definitions of " approved school " and " remand home ".
1961 c. 39.	The Criminal Justice Act 1961.	In section 1, subsection (1) and the proviso to subsection (2). In section 4, in subsection (1) the words " but not less than fourteen ", and in subsection (2)(*a*) the words from " the offender " to " and ". In section 5(2), paragraph (*a*) and the words following paragraph (*b*), and section 5(3). In section 6, subsections (1) and (2), and in subsection (3) the words from " or ordering " to " home " in paragraph (*a*), the words from " or " to " home " in paragraph (*b*), and the words " or remand home " and " a prison is so named and ". In section 7, subsection (2), and in subsection (3) the words from " and where " onwards.

Chapter	Short title	Extent of repeal
1961 c. 39— *cont.*	The Criminal Justice Act 1961—*cont.*	Section 8(1) and (2). In section 9, paragraph (*a*). In section 10(2)(*a*), the words from " except " to " excessive ". Sections 14 to 19, 22(4) and 25. In section 29(1), the words " remand home " and " special reception centre or other " and in section 29(3) the words from " special " to " 1933 and ". Schedule 2. In Schedule 4 the entries relating to sections 54, 72, 78, 82, 83 and 88 of the Act of 1933 and to Schedule 4 to that Act and the entries relating to the Children and Young Persons Act 1938, section 72 and the change in the definition of " sentence " in section 80(1) of the Criminal Justice Act 1948, sections 20 and 32 of the Magistrates' Courts Act 1952, and section 79 of the Mental Health Act 1959.
1963 c. 33.	The London Government Act 1963.	In section 47, in subsection (1) the words " and in the definition of ' remand home ' in any enactment ", and in subsection (3) the reference in paragraph (*c*) to section 49 of the Criminal Justice Act 1948. In Schedule 17, paragraph 18(*c*).
1963 c. 37.	The Children and Young Persons Act 1963.	Sections 1(4), 2 and 4 to 15. Section 22. In section 23, in subsection (1), paragraph (*a*) and the word " authority ", subsection (2), in subsection (3) the words " or subsection (2) " in both places and the words " takes refuge there or ", and subsections (6) to (8). Section 24. In section 25(1) the words " or taken to a place of safety ", and section 25(2). In section 29, in subsection (1) the words " continue to " and subsection (2). Section 33. Section 53(1) and (2).

Chapter	Short title	Extent of repeal
1963 c. 37— *cont.*	The Children and Young Persons Act 1963—*cont.*	In section 55 the words from " section 84(5) " to " principal Act ", the word " or " immediately preceding the words " section 17 " and the words from " (which relate " onwards. Sections 59 and 61. In section 65(5), the words " subsections (1) and (2) of section 10 and ", " and 53(1) " and " 27 " and " 34 ". Schedule 1. In Schedule 3, paragraphs 10, 15 to 23, 25 to 27, 33, 34, 35, 36, 44, 46, 48 and 49, and in paragraph 50 the words " special reception centre or other ", and " ' special reception centre ' has the same meaning as in the Children and Young Persons Act 1933 and ".
1963 c. 39.	The Criminal Justice (Scotland) Act 1963.	In Schedule 5, the entry relating to the Children Act 1948.
1965 c. 53.	The Family Allowances Act 1965.	In section 11(1), sub-paragraph (i) of paragraph (*a*) and in paragraph (*c*) the words from " made " to " order ".
1967 c. 80.	The Criminal Justice Act 1967.	In section 55, the words " or any provision of the Children and Young Persons Act 1933" and the words from " and accordingly " onwards. In section 77(1), the words " on his means ". In Part I of Schedule 3, the entries relating to sections 72(5) and 82(5) of the Act of 1933 and section 14 of the Act of 1963.
1968 c. 49.	The Social Work (Scotland) Act 1968.	In section 72(2), the words " of the Children and Young Persons Acts 1933 to 1963 or, as the case may be ", the word " respectively " and the words " to a supervision order within the meaning of section 5 of the Children and Young Persons Act 1963 or ". In section 73(2), the word " juvenile ". In section 74, in subsection (3) the words " in England or Wales or " and " if he thinks fit " and the words from " an approved " to " be " where it

SCH. 6

Chapter	Short title	Extent of repeal
1968 c. 49—*cont.*	The Social Work (Scotland) Act 1968—*cont.*	first occurs, in subsection (4) the words from " the Children " to " be of ", the words " an approved school or " in the first, second and third places where they occur, the word " of " and " in " following those words in the first and third of those places respectively and the words " section 71 of the said Act of 1933 or " and " section 90 of the said Act of 1933 or under ", and in subsection (5) the words " of the Acts of 1933 to 1963 or, as the case may be ", the words " of a local authority or, as the case may be " and the words " those Acts or ". In section 75, in subsection (1) the words " the Secretary of State or " and " approved school or ", and in subsection (3) the words " approved school or ". In section 76, in subsections (1) and (2) the word " juvenile " wherever it occurs, and in subsection (4) the words " approved school or " and " of the approved school or ". Section 77(1)(*b*). In section 90(1) the words " or to prescribe any matter ". In Schedule 2, in paragraph 10 the words from " and " to " 1933 ". In Schedule 8, paragraphs 2 to 5, 18, 21 and 35.

SCHEDULE 7

SECTIONS 1 TO 6 AND 14 OF THE CHILDREN ACT 1958 AS AMENDED

Section 72(5).

1958 c. 65.

1. It shall be the duty of every local authority to satisfy themselves as to the well-being of children within their area who are foster children within the meaning of this Part of this Act and, for that purpose, to secure that, so far as appears to the authority to be appropriate, the children are visited from time to time by officers of the authority and that such advice is given as to the care and maintenance of the children as appears to be needed.

Duty of local authorities to ensure well-being of foster children.

2.—(1) In this Part of this Act " foster child " means, subject to the following provisions of this section, a child below the upper limit of the compulsory school age whose care and maintenance are undertaken by a person who is not a relative or guardian of his.

(2) A child is not a foster child within the meaning of this Part of this Act while he is in the care of a local authority or a voluntary organisation or is boarded out by a local health authority or a local education authority (or, in Scotland, an education authority).

(3) A child is not a foster child within the meaning of this Part of this Act while he is in the care of any person—

(*a*) in premises in which any parent, adult relative or guardian of his is for the time being residing ;

(*b*) in any voluntary home within the meaning of Part V of the Children and Young Persons Act, 1933, or in any residential establishment within the meaning of the Social Work (Scotland) Act 1968 ;

(*c*) in any school within the meaning of the Education Acts, 1944 to 1953, or the Education (Scotland) Acts 1939 to 1956 in which he is receiving full-time education ;

(*d*) in any hospital or in any nursing home registered or exempted from registration under Part VI of the Public Health Act, 1936, Part XI of the Public Health (London) Act, 1936, or the Nursing Homes Registration (Scotland) Act, 1938 ; or

(*e*) in any home or institution not specified in this section but maintained by a public or local authority.

(3A) A child is not a foster child within the meaning of this Part of this Act at any time while his care and maintenance are undertaken by a person, other than a relative or guardian of his, if at that time—

(*a*) that person does not intend to, and does not in fact, under-take his care and maintenance for a continuous period of more than six days ; or

(*b*) that person is not a regular foster parent and does not intend to, and does not in fact, undertake his care and maintenance for a continuous period of more than twenty-seven days ;

and for the purposes of this subsection a person is a regular foster parent if, during the period of twelve months immediately pre-ceding the date on which he begins to undertake the care and main-tenance of the child in question, he had, otherwise than as a relative or guardian, the care and maintenance of one or more children either for a period of, or periods amounting in the aggregate to, not less than three months or for at least three continuous periods each of which was of more than six days.

(4) A child is not a foster child within the meaning of this Part of this Act while he is in the care of any person in compliance with a supervision order within the meaning of the Children and

Young Persons Act 1969 or a probation order or supervision requirement or by virtue of a fit person order or while he is in an approved
school or is deemed for the purposes of the Children and Young
Persons (Scotland) Act, 1937, to be under the care of the managers
of an approved school or while he is liable to be detained or subject
to guardianship under the Mental Health Act, 1959, or the Mental
Health (Scotland) Act, 1960, or is resident in a residential home for
mentally disordered persons within the meaning of Part III of the
Mental Health Act, 1959, or in a residential home for persons suffering from mental disorder within the meaning of Part III of the
Mental Health (Scotland) Act, 1960.

(4A) A child is not a foster child for the purposes of this Part
of this Act while he is placed in the care and possession of a
person who proposes to adopt him under arrangements made by
such a local authority or registered adoption society as is referred
to in Part II of the Adoption Act 1958 or while he is a protected
child within the meaning of Part IV of that Act.

3.—(1) Subject to the following provisions of this section, a
person who proposes to maintain as a foster child a child not
already in his care shall give written notice thereof to the local
authority not less than two weeks and not more than four weeks
before he receives the child, unless he receives him in an emergency;
and a person who maintains a foster child whom he received in
an emergency or who became a foster child while in his care shall
give written notice thereof to the local authority not later than forty-
eight hours after he receives the child or, as the case may be, after
the child becomes a foster child.

Duty of person maintaining foster children to notify local authority.

(2) Every such notice shall specify the date on which it is intended
that the child should be received or, as the case may be, on which
the child was in fact received or became a foster child and the
premises in which the child is to be or is being kept and shall be
given to the local authority for the area in which those premises
are situated.

(2A) A person shall not be required to give notice under subsection (1) of this section in relation to a child if—

   (*a*) he has on a previous occasion given notice under that subsection in respect of that or any other child, specifying the
   premises at which he proposes to keep the child in question; and

   (*b*) he has not, at any time since that notice was given, ceased
   to maintain at least one foster child at those premises and
   been required by virtue of the following provisions of this
   section to give notice under subsection (5A) of this section
   in respect of those premises.

(3) Where a person who is maintaining one or more foster
children changes his permanent address or the premises in which the
child is, or the children are, kept he shall, not less than two weeks
and not more than four weeks before the change or, if the change
is made in an emergency, not later than forty-eight hours after the
change, give written notice to the said local authority, specifying
the new address or premises, and if the new premises are in the

area of another local authority, the authority to whom the notice is given shall inform that other local authority and give them such of the particulars mentioned in subsection (7) of this section as are known to them.

(4) If a foster child dies the person who was maintaining him shall, within forty-eight hours thereof, give to the local authority and to the person from whom the child was received notice in writing of the death.

(5) Where a foster child is removed or removes himself from the care of the person maintaining him, that person shall at the request of the local authority give them the name and address, if known, of the person (if any) into whose care the child has been removed.

(5A) Subject to the provisions of the following subsection, where a person who has been maintaining one or more foster children at any premises ceases to maintain foster children at those premises and the circumstances are such that no notice is required to be given under subsection (3) or subsection (4) of this section, that person shall, within forty-eight hours after he ceases to maintain any foster child at those premises, give notice in writing thereof to the local authority.

(5B) A person need not give the notice required by the preceding subsection in consequence of his ceasing to maintain foster children at any premises if, at the time he so ceases, he intends within twenty-seven days again to maintain any of them as a foster child at those premises ; but if he subsequently abandons that intention or the said period expires without his having given effect to it he shall give the said notice within forty-eight hours of that event.

(7) A person maintaining or proposing to maintain a foster child shall at the request of the local authority give them the following particulars, so far as known to him, that is to say, the name, sex, and date and place of birth of the child, and the name and address of every person who is a parent or guardian or acts as a guardian of the child or from whom the child has been or is to be received.

Power to inspect premises, impose conditions, or prohibit the keeping of foster children.

4.—(1) Any officer of a local authority authorised to visit foster children may, after producing, if asked to do so, some duly authenticated document showing that he is so authorised, inspect any premises in the area of the authority in the whole or any part of which foster children are to be or are being kept.

(1A) If it is shown to the satisfaction of a justice of the peace on sworn information in writing—

(a) that there is reasonable cause to believe that a foster child is being kept in any premises, or in any part thereof ; and

(b) that admission to those premises or that part thereof has been refused to a duly authorised officer of the local authority or that such a refusal is apprehended or that the occupier is temporarily absent,

the justice may by warrant under his hand authorise an officer of the local authority to enter the premises if need be by force, at any reasonable time within forty-eight hours of the issue of the warrant, for the purpose of inspecting the premises.

(2) Where a person is keeping or proposes to keep foster children in premises used (while foster children are kept therein) wholly or partly for that purpose, the local authority may impose on him requirements, to be complied with, after such time as the authority may specify, whenever a foster child is kept in the premises, as to—

(a) the number, age and sex of the foster children who may be kept at any one time in the premises or any part thereof;

(b) the accommodation and equipment to be provided for the children;

(c) the medical arrangements to be made for protecting the health of the children;

(d) the giving of particulars of the person for the time being in charge of the children;

(e) the number, qualifications or experience of the persons employed in looking after the children;

(f) the keeping of records;

(g) the fire precautions to be taken in the premises;

(h) the giving of particulars of any foster child received in the premises and of any change in the number or identity of the foster children kept therein;

but any such requirement may be limited to a particular class of foster children kept in the premises and any requirement imposed under paragraphs (b) to (h) of this subsection may be limited by the authority so as to apply only when the number of foster children kept in the premises exceeds a specified number.

(3) Where a person proposes to keep a foster child in any premises and the local authority are of the opinion that—

(a) the premises are not suitable premises in which to keep foster children; or

(b) that person is not a suitable person to have the care and maintenance of foster children; or

(c) it would be detrimental to that child to be kept by that person in those premises;

the local authority may impose a prohibition on that person under subsection (3A) of this section.

(3A) A prohibition imposed on any person under this subsection may—

(a) prohibit him from keeping any foster child in premises specified in the prohibition; or

(b) prohibit him from keeping any foster child in any premises in the area of the local authority; or

(c) prohibit him from keeping a particular child specified in the prohibition in premises so specified.

(3B) Where a local authority have imposed a prohibition on any person under subsection (3A) of this section, the local authority may, if they think fit, cancel the prohibition, either of their own motion or on an application made by that person on the ground of a change in the circumstances in which a foster child would be kept by him.

(4) Where a local authority impose a requirement on any person under subsection (2) of this section as respects any premises, they may prohibit him from keeping foster children in the premises after the time specified for compliance with the requirement unless the requirement is complied with.

(5) Any requirement or prohibition imposed under this section shall be imposed by notice in writing addressed to the person on whom it is imposed.

Appeal to juvenile court against requirement or prohibition imposed under section four.

5.—(1) Any person aggrieved by any requirement or prohibition imposed under section four of this Act may, within fourteen days from the date on which he is notified of the requirement or prohibition, or, in the case of a prohibition imposed under subsection (3A) of that section, within fourteen days from the refusal by the local authority to accede to an application by him for the cancellation of the prohibition, appeal to a juvenile court, and where the appeal is against such a requirement the requirement shall not have effect while the appeal is pending.

(2) Where the court allows such an appeal it may, instead of cancelling the requirement or prohibition, vary the requirement or allow more time for compliance with it or, where an absolute prohibition has been imposed, substitute for it a prohibition to use the premises after such time as the court may specify unless such specified requirements as the local authority had power to impose under section four of this Act are complied with.

(3) Any notice by which a requirement or prohibition is imposed on any person under section four of this Act shall contain a statement informing him of his right to appeal against the requirement or prohibition and of the time within which he may do so.

(4) Any requirement or prohibition specified or substituted under this section by the court shall be deemed for the purposes of this Part of this Act other than this section to have been imposed by the local authority under section four of this Act.

(5) In the application of this section to Scotland, for references to a juvenile court there shall be substituted references to the sheriff.

Disqualification for keeping foster children.

6.—(1) A person shall not maintain a foster child if—

    (*a*) an order has been made against him under this Part of this Act removing a child from his care ;

    (*b*) an order has been made under the Children and Young Persons Act, 1933, the Children and Young Persons Act 1969, or the Children and Young Persons (Scotland) Act, 1937, or a supervision requirement has been made under the Social Work (Scotland) Act 1968 and by virtue of the order or requirement a child was removed from his care ;

SCH. 7

(c) he has been convicted of any offence specified in the First Schedule to the said Act of 1933 or the First Schedule to the said Act of 1937 or has been placed on probation or discharged absolutely or conditionally for any such offence;

(d) his rights and powers with respect to a child have been vested in a local authority under section two of the Children Act, 1948 or under section 16 of the Social Work (Scotland) Act 1968;

(e) a local health authority or in Scotland a local authority have made an order under subsection (3) or (4) of section one of the Nurseries and Child-Minders Regulation Act 1948 refusing, or an order under section five of that Act cancelling, the registration of any premises occupied by him or his registration;

(f) an order has been made under section 43 of the Adoption Act 1958 for the removal of a protected child who was being kept or was about to be received by him,

unless he has disclosed that fact to the local authority and obtained their consent.

(2) Where this section applies to any person, otherwise than by virtue of this subsection, it shall apply also to any other person who lives in the same premises as he does or who lives in premises at which he is employed.

14.—(1) A person shall be guilty of an offence if— Offences.

(a) being required, under any provision of this Part of this Act, to give any notice or information, he fails to give the notice within the time specified in that provision or fails to give the information within a reasonable time, or knowingly makes or causes or procures another person to make any false or misleading statement in the notice or information;

(b) he refuses to allow the visiting of any foster child by a duly authorised officer of a local authority or the inspection, under the power conferred by subsection (1) of section four of this Act, of any premises or wilfully obstructs a person entitled to enter any premises by virtue of a warrant under subsection (1A) of that section;

(c) he fails to comply with any requirement imposed by a local authority under this Part of this Act or keeps any foster child in any premises in contravention of a prohibition so imposed;

(d) he maintains a foster child in contravention of section six of this Act; or

(e) he refuses to comply with an order under this Part of this Act for the removal of any child or obstructs any person in the execution of such an order.

(1A) Where section 6 of this Act applies to any person by virtue only of subsection (2) of that section, he shall not be guilty of an offence under paragraph (d) of subsection (1) of this section

SCH. 7   if he proves that he did not know, and had no reasonable ground for believing, that a person living or employed in the premises in which he lives was a person to whom that section applies.

(2) A person guilty of an offence under this section shall be liable on summary conviction to imprisonment for a term not exceeding six months or a fine not exceeding one hundred pounds or both.

(2A) If any person who is required, under any provision of this Part of this Act, to give a notice fails to give the notice within the time specified in that provision, then, notwithstanding anything in section 104 of the Magistrates' Courts Act 1952 (time limit for proceedings) proceedings for the offence may be brought at any time within six months from the date when evidence of the offence came to the knowledge of the local authority.

(3) In England and Wales, a local authority may institute proceedings for an offence under this section.

PRODUCED IN ENGLAND BY COMMERCIAL COLOUR PRESS LONDON
FOR BERNARD M THIMONT
Controller of Her Majesty's Stationery Office and Queen's Printer of Acts of Parliament